NAMING
THE WAVES

NAMING THE WAVES

Contemporary Lesbian Poetry

Edited by Christian McEwen

The Crossing Press
Freedom, California

For Gloria Anzaldú, teacher extraordinary

Library of Congress Cataloging-in-Publication Data

Naming the waves : contemporary lesbian poetry / edited by Christian
    McEwen.
        p.   cm.
    "British edition 1988 by Virago Press Limited"—T.p. verso.
    ISBN 0-89594-371-9 — ISBN 0-89594-370-0 (pbk.)
    1. Lesbians—Poetry. 2. Lesbians' writings, American.
3. Lesbians' writings, English. 4. American poetry—20th century.
5. English poetry—20th century.   I. McEwen, Christian, 1956- .
PS595.L46N36   1988
811'.54080353—dc20   89-17303
                                                          CIP

Contents ✍

Acknowledgements

When I look back over what it has meant to put this book together, my overriding feeling is tremendous gratitude. I was helped first and foremost by Jane Winter, who loved and listened to me throughout, and who, for six months in New York, paid my share of the rent, leaving me free to work part time. On the east coast I was helped by Mary Allgier, Malaga Baldi, Nancy Bereano, Jan Clausen, Deborah Edel and Bea Gates, by Marilyn Hacker, Joan Larkin, Joan Nestle and Susan Sherman; on the west coast by Gloria Anzaldúa and Irena Klepfisz; and in London by Lilian Mohin, Ruthie Petrie and Alison Read, all of whom gave me names, information and support. Laetitia Bermejo, Sharon Franklet, Janice Gould, Simon Korner, Andrea Loewenstein, Maia, Isabella McEwen, Aurora Levins Morales, Leonie Rushforth, Elizabeth Tallent and Anne Witten sent, as always, love and mail from places far away. In daily life there were Roz Calvert, Deborah Kaufmann, Maria Margaronis, Donna Masini and Lisa Vice, all of whom I knew I could always call. And then there were the poems and the poets themselves. Many, many thanks.

Many of the poems in this collection have not been published previously; I am grateful to each of the poets for agreeing to have her work printed here.

For permission to reprint material that has appeared elsewhere, grateful acknowledgements are as follows: Beth Allen, 'Lovesuit', copyright © 1979 by Beth Allen, in *Sappho VII/2*; Dorothy Allison, 'To the Bone', 'Not Speaking, Screaming', 'Whoring Away My Imagination', 'Little Enough', copyright © 1983 by Dorothy Allison, from *The Women Who Hate Me* (Long Haul Press, now available from Firebrand Books); Jane Barnes, 'No', 'I Want You', 'Homophobia', copyright © by Jane Barnes, from *Extremes* (Blue Giant Press); Judith Barrington, 'Naming the Waves', 'Passing', 'Lesbian', copyright © 1985 by Judith Barrington, from *Trying to be an Honest Woman* (The Eighth Mountain Press); Robin Becker, 'A Good Education', 'When Friends Leave', and 'On Not Being Able to Imagine the Future', copyright © 1982 by Robin Becker, from *Backtalk* (Alice James Press); Beth Brant, 'Her Name is Helen', copyright © 1985 by Beth Brant, from *Mohawk Trail* (Firebrand Books); Olga Broumas, 'Little Red Riding Hood', copyright © 1977 by Olga Broumas, from *Beginning With O* (Yale University Press); 'Landscape With Next of Kin', copyright © 1979 by Olga Broumas, from *Soie Sauvage* (Copper Canyon Press); Roz Calvert,

Introduction

Naming the Waves is a collection of transatlantic lesbian poetry, roughly half of which is British and half North American. It is arranged alphabetically according to first name (in the case of writers who have used first name only) or last name (in the case of everyone else), thus creating a benign confusion about who comes from where. Having lived in both countries, I know very well that poets who are household names on one side of the ocean are often quite unheard of on the other. Instead of emphasising this by setting up an us/them, US/UK dichotomy, I have chosen to let each writer speak for herself, claiming an identity in the terms that she herself prefers.

'We are done with feeling all the same,' writes Judith Barrington in the title poem, 'done with that blind joy/of sudden recognition/womanness alone will not get us through'. She looks back with some regret to the early days of consciousness-raising, when it was enough (or seemed enough) simply to be female. These days, 'Our differences are like the oceans', and they cannot be ignored.

Atlantic grey is not
Pacific green-grey is not
Aegean clear green.

It is in fact exactly this naming and claiming and celebrating of difference which has preoccupied feminists in recent years. As it expands beyond the narrowness of its white middle-class founding mothers, the women's movement changes, it becomes fiercer and stronger and more and more unpredictable.[1] The naming that is being done is not the anxious and patronising labelling of one group of people by another (Blacks by whites, gays by straights, women by men, working class by upper class). It is naming in the sense of recognising, giving form to what was always there.

There are places . . .
where patterns in the water
guiding sailors
have names in certain languages

Each year there are more of those languages, and they are used with greater authority and self-confidence. In *Naming the Waves*, many of the writers are new, some have never been published before. There are older and younger women, mothers and co-mothers, single women and women with partners. Race and background vary too, as even a quick glance at the biographies will reveal.

As I worked on the book, reading, researching, opening stacks of envelopes every day, I was never able to forget that fact, or to submerge those differences – and different languages – under some simple literary criterion of 'good writing'. I think I tried to, lots of times. But the poetry itself resisted me. It tested me and asked me questions. What was I looking for? What did I think was good? And why was I so rude about the three most common kinds of submission: the right-on-dyke oppression poem, the cunt glorification poem, and the weepy lyrics of abandonment? Did these indeed constitute the broken heart of lesbian poetry?

I kept on reading, and I found a thousand answers to those questions, all of them provisional. I found poems which upset and disturbed me, poems I knew I'd read again and again, and others which I didn't even like. Content, style and emphasis might vary, but even so, I felt I recognised each book-poem as I encountered it. 'You belong in the anthology – and you – and you –' It was as if they were all part of the same endeavour, some tremendous telling of important truths. When I tried to explain to myself what I meant by this, one image in particular would reappear. It was the child with the world in her pocket from Roz Calvert's poem, 'Get Over':

> She watched closely
> the hole in her pocket
> so the world would not fall out
> . . .
> Squeezed it in her warm hand
> saying . . . Someday
> not now
> gotta hide it
> so no one think I stole it
> But someday
> I get down the street
> around the corner
> lemme take it out
> lemme have a looksee

Each of the poets I was reading had a different 'world in her pocket', and each of them was writing at least partly for the reason Calvert gave, 'lemme take it out/lemme have a looksee'. Her poem was perhaps especially important to me because it was written in the voice of a child, and I had learned to trust that voice, both in myself and in my friends. Once alerted, I began to hear in recent lesbian writing something like a children's crusade. Roz Calvert's eager, anxious little girl was not the only one. Linda Smukler, Nina Newington and Joan Larkin had all written of that child; and Adrienne Rich has spoken of her too:

> The child's soul musters strength
> where the holes were torn

For years those children had kept their secrets to themselves ('someday/not now/gotta hide it'). Now, at last, they were beginning to speak up, to try to make their voices heard over the confident pronouncements of the grownups (substitute *whites*, substitute *straight people, rich people, people with power, the literary establishment, the middle class*). They were trying to tell what they saw as the truth, and the grownups were refusing to believe them. In her poem 'The Lesbian Divorce', Rebecca Lewin makes this agonisingly clear:

> *I can't say to the world, Help me, I am divorced,*
> I am divorced!

> *They would not even believe*
> *we had ever been married.*

It is this difficulty we live with, this wall which suddenly appears where no wall was, that kindly straight friends find it hardest to believe in. It is easier, perhaps, to understand (and mock) the obviously ridiculous stereotypes,[2] or to face the righteous hatred of a phalanx of Middle American Christians, all with banners proclaiming, 'GOD LOVES YOU BUT HATES YOUR SINS, PARAIDS LEAD TO SICKNESS AND DEATH'[3] than it is to piece together the smaller hostilities: the joke which is smothered when the lesbian comes in, the sudden lack of trust, the snide social references. Yet those tiny things, repeated daily, are often the most painful ones to bear: *'They would not believe/ we had ever been married'*. It is not marriage that is at issue here, but human credibility. When that is refused, lesbians have to find other ways to protect ourselves. What does it do to you when the people you love most cannot be talked about, when every little happening must be reshuffled and differently emphasised, and all the pronouns changed? There are photographs missing from this book, surnames altered. Some women have found it necessary to use a pseudonym. Some, I know, have not allowed themselves to be included.

Until recently, lesbian poetry was very much expected to wear its heart on its sleeve (or its identity on its lapel). It was thought of mainly as love poetry, or poetry written in answer to oppression.[4] Nowadays, this is beginning to change. The most interesting work is being done neither out of innocence, nor in self-defence, but at a point slightly beyond, where the clear-eyed child and the outraged adult start to merge. The literary creature who results is perhaps no more than an ideal of my own. (Though indeed I've seen her up there on the platform, I have heard her read. She has many faces, and she shows herself in many different ways.) But always she acts in the knowledge of her own past pain and of the harm that it has done, and always she uses that knowledge to generate a new, more responsible kind of behaviour. This is never an easy thing to do. As Audre Lorde says in her poem, 'Stations':

> *Some women love*
> *to wait*
> *for life   for a ring*
> *in the June light   for a touch*
> *of the sun to heal them   or another*
> *woman's voice   to make them whole*

We are all of us tempted to leave the work to someone else. But the truth is, it does no good to *wait for yourself around the next corner and call the empty spot peace*. No voice other than your own can make you whole. The writers in this book are very clear about this. They are using their voices – their poems – as a way of making choices in the world. As Audre Lorde, again, says so well in one of her essays, '[poetry] forms the quality of light within which we predicate our hopes and dreams towards survival and change, first made into language, then into idea, then into more tangible action.'[5]

More often than not, this taking action begins with self-description, moving, as many of these poems do, through the different stages of a woman's life. It would be easy to pursue this theme throughout the book, starting with such poems as Pat Parker's 'Group' or Nina Newington's 'Poem for Jackie' which try in some ways to confront the past, and moving on through those that deal with the present and the difficult acquisition of self-love. Here I think of Caroline Griffin's 'Call This A Life Lived Backwards', and Caroline Halliday's 'smell of myself', a model for me of affectionate self-appreciation, by no means lightly won.

> *Little children don't have the wrinkled thin labia I have, they have round fat curves. R's as marked out and smiling as a mouth . . . a cheerful fanny.*
>
> *I touched my arsehole yesterday to sniff my fingers . . .*
>
> *Light robust comfortable smell.*

This self-celebration reappears,[6] and, once established, expands naturally into poems of love and friendship and coalition: Marg Yeo's 'leaves and potatoes', for example, with its unexpected echoes of e.e. cummings:

> *when I think*
> *of her it is*
> *thin   but*
> *solid and potato*
> *simple*
> *   and sudden with leaves in*
> *side and*
> *everywhere*[7]

Then too, there are the mother/daughter poems,[8] and the poems of lesbian motherhood (see especially, Eve Featherstone's 'There Were Three In the Bed'),[9] as well as the poems of work and overwork, and the poems of no work at all, among them Gudrun Fonfa's 'Welfare Was My Husband' with its wonderfully contemptuous lines:

> *Do I miss your no face*
> *your cheshire cat cock?*
> *Do I miss your little*
> *late checks?*

In reading this, the littleness of the checks (cheques!) follows so soon after the 'cheshire cat cock' that the two things somehow exchange attributes: the checks vanishing in no time at all, and Fonfa, in consequence, taunting Welfare with the size of his penis. This is fighting stuff, boisterous, accurate, *feisty*, an American word which has no exact British equivalent. It is the voice of the child grown up and on her feet, the child who knows now where the trouble starts, and who to trust and where to turn for help.

In trying to describe this, I by no means want to imply that the voice is a homogeneous one, nor that 'appropriate concerns' are to any degree laid down in advance. There are as many ways of taking power as there are poets writing. Janice Gould is not Sapphire is not Audre Lorde, though all three write about the politics of identity: Lorde as a Black woman, Sapphire as a fat one, and Gould as a Native American. To do this well and forcefully, and not at the same time to antagonise all readers who belong to other categories, is something that requires great skill. Both writer and reader must be able to stand their own ground without feeling that everyone else stands (or ought to stand) beside them. '*If their anger frightens you, try to understand their grief*', as Honor Moore says so wisely in 'Spuyten Duyvil'.[10] That is what it means to welcome difference.

There is no doubt that this welcoming of difference, really acknowledging it, and still really welcoming it, is one of the hardest tasks that feminists have taken on. In her long poem, 'there is a woman in our town', Pat Parker writes of all the women who get left out of the usual versions of sisterhood: the drinker, the wife, the fat woman, the business woman, the mental health survivor, the drug addict. 'Is she our sister?' she asks in her refrain. We chorus eagerly that of course she is, but putting that 'of course' into practice is another matter. The lesbian community can be a hard church to belong to: a self-righteous, narrow-minded cruel place. It can also be astonishing in its support and openness, strangers reaching out to welcome strangers, glad of the chance to 'hear each other into speech'.[11] In the making of this book, I began to look very deliberately for work which moved towards that particular generosity of spirit. It was for this reason that I asked to include Judy Grahn's 'Paris and Helen', a deeply romantic poem of heterosexual love:

> *He called her: golden dawn*
> *She called him: the wind whistles*
>
> *He called her: heart of the sky*
> *She called him: message bringer*

To paraphrase Grahn herself, the true definition of an act of indecency is an act of omission.[12] This being so, the truly moral, truly committed act must be *to include*.[13]

Beyond the poetry of identity politics is the poetry of inclusiveness. Judith Macdaniel's 'La Esperanza' is such a poem, as is Audre Lorde's 'Ethiopia':

Seven years without milk
means that everyone dances for joy
on your birthday
but when you clap   your hands
break at the wrist
and even grandmother's ghee
cannot mend
the delicate embroideries
of bone

There is no rant here, no war or glory-mongering on the part of the poet; everything is given over to the simple recounting of the event. The same is true of Irena Klepfisz's 'From the Monkey House and Other Cages', which tells the story of two female monkeys in the monkey house at the zoo. In the course of this poem, Klepfisz manages to move from and beyond the monkeys to include all alienated lives and unwanted separations, human as well as animal. Her language is charged, both morally and technically. Few poets speak with such authority.

Any writer's authority is, of course, to some degree dependent on the form in which she chooses to write, and it is interesting to see how many forms are now being tried. For a long time, the distrust of male-dominated academia meant that women, if they did write in forms, tended to go for those they perceived as simpler and less contaminated; the influence of the chant, the rant, the fairy tale and nursery rhyme were strong. See, for example, Roz Calvert's 'Crack Corn', where a folksong and a children's chant are successfully and defiantly blended in a poem about father/daughter incest. See, too, her 'Marilyn' with its easy conversational rhythms, a poem in which female love-making is described with the utmost economy and in terms no one could fail to understand, the two women literally merging in the body of one (plural) noun, as they *'fall into bed like a woman and a man/like a woman and a woman/like two women.'*

Beyond and alongside these older solutions has come another kind of writing, a mastery of the so-called 'male' techniques: the sestina, the sonnet, the villanelle. Marilyn Hacker is the acknowledged leader of this more formal school, but there are other, younger writers following in her tracks.[14] Then too, in a category which still needs definition, there is the experimental prose-poetry of such writers as Sharon Franklet, here represented by her shameless and surreal 'cunt poem':

> *i use both hands, holding the sack in my lap like a cat, running my hands down its inside, till they meet moist and pungent in the seepage at the bottom. She feels like seagrass massed together, like dying sodden leaves, like oysters and mussels raw in the strainer*[15]

There is an excitement here, an honesty and originality and a freedom to experiment, which I associate with the *grandes dames* of lesbian literature, most obviously, perhaps, with Gertrude Stein. Like the work of Judy Grahn and Adrienne Rich, like Irena Klepfisz's bilingual Yiddish/English poems ('Fradel Schtok' and 'A Few Words in the Mother Tongue'), this is a poetry for which there is no substitute, a language (or languages) invented because nothing else will do. As listeners, we are hungry to receive it. We know each other's voices now. We read each other's books. 'Tell me the story/again,' says Joan Larkin in her poem 'Thread', and it is the question that every writer wants to hear. *So then what happened? Go on, tell me more –*

Notes

1. See, for example, *This Bridge Called My Back: Writings By Radical Women of Color*, Ed. Cherrie Moraga and Gloria Anzaldúa, Persephone Press, 1982.
2. See Caroline Claxton's poem, 'Lesbian: Your Image', p. 30, with its list of stereotypes, including 'left-wing-commie-cigar-smoking-butch-bulldykes-against-the-bomb'.
3. These people were actually present at the New York City Gay and Lesbian Parade, 29 June 1986. It was a curious experience to meet their outrage and contempt head on – and to know at the same time that they all believed themselves the followers of a god of love.
4. See, among others, poems by Jane Barnes, 'Homophobia', p. 6, Maria Jastrzębska, 'Seeing the Pope on TV', p. 84, Kim, 'Lesbian Strength', p. 96, and Linda King, 'Spotting Lesbian Socks', p. 97.
5. Audre Lorde, *Sister/Outsider*, p. 37, The Crossing Press, New York, 1984.
6. See Bea Gates, 'Conversation With The Body', p. 52, its animal image replicated in Halliday's 'This Space the Tiger', p. 78.
7. See also Sapphire's 'i guess if i was a sound', p. 184, and Minnie Bruce Pratt's 'Waulking Song II', p. 158, and 'Not A Gun, Not A Knife', p. 164.
8. I think here of Olga Broumas' 'Little Red Riding Hood', p. 16, Marilyn Hacker's 'Mother II', p. 72 and Janice Gould's 'We Exist', p. 57.

9. See also Meg Kelly's 'The Bogeywoman', p. 93, and Helen Ramsbottom's 'Lesbians and Mothers', p. 164, among others.

10. See also Dorothy Allison's 'Whoring Away My Imagination', p. 2.

11. See Nelle Morton in 'Beloved Image!', paper delivered at the National Conference of the American Academy of Religion, San Francisco, California, December 28, 1977, quoted in *Lies, Secrets and Silence* by Adrienne Rich, Norton & Co., 1979.

12. See section 4 of Judy Grahn's long poem, 'A Woman Is Talking To Death', p. 62.

13. It was for this reason that I asked for Jan Clausen's 'Apostate', p. 29, as well as Mary Dorcey's 'Drunken Truths', p. 32, which some will find dangerously nostalgic.

14. See Jan Clausen's 'Sestina, Winchell's Donut House', p. 28, and Jennifer Rose, 'At Dachau With a German Lover', p. 177.

15. See Sharon Franklet's 'cunt poem', p. 50, the secret subject of so many lesbian poems. For another powerful example, see Elana Dykewomon's 'Even My Eyes Become Mouths', p. 37.

Beth Allen ✍

LOVESUIT

When at first we loved
And lay so quiet together,
It was like I'd drawn
The zipper in your skin and climbed
Inside. My legs and feet filled
Gaps between your bones.
My arms pushed and stretched
Through yours, like sleeves, to the finger
Ends. I snuggled there beneath
Your skin, and stilled. You slid
The zipper back and we were one.

Dorothy Allison ✍

TO THE BONE

That summer I did not go crazy,
spoke instead to my mama who insisted
our people do not go crazy.
We make instead that sudden evening
silence that follows the shotgun blast.
We stand up alone twenty years after
like a scarecrow in a field
pie-eyed, toothless, naming
our enemies and outliving them.
That summer I talked to death
like an old friend, a husky voice
whispering up from my cunt, echoing
around my knees, laughing.
That summer I did not go crazy
but I wore

         very close

very close

         to the bone.

NOT SPEAKING, SCREAMING

Silence is *the* problem,
she said.   She insisted.
I went for a walk in the grey morning
up Seventh Avenue toward the park
with the pigeons and the Boarshead delivery men.
On every block someone camped,
some mottled grey face shivered
settled in a bed of trash.

Have you noticed the sudden increase
in shoeshine stands? I asked her.
She kept her hands in her pockets,
her chin fierce.   No.
I pulled my silence in around me,
remembered years disappearing
because I would not speak of them.
You're right, of course, I told her,
gave in,   fell silent,
thinking still of that tall woman
who walks Broadway with such long steps
and screams
and screams.

WHORING AWAY MY IMAGINATION

Mama wants me rich and famous.
An old lover keeps asking me when the hell
am I going to write that bestseller anyway?
I shrug. She has read so much of my work,
still never understands how the work
has its own rhythm, its own needs, how
sometimes I swear I'm transcribing, living
my life around the work not through it.
That other lover, the one followed me all those weeks
threatening to deliver me just the adventure I deserved,
she's saved all my letters, stories, poems;
plans on being famous shortly after me,
which is almost as funny as the one who wanted
me to pay her not to send the same stuff
to my boss.   So send it, I said.

Sitting down over work never seems
to get finished, head nodding exhausted
after eight hours of other people's typing,
typing my own journal-poems, short stories,
and those three novels never come to an end,
I pick up speed going nowhere
trying to hang onto the wider view
my life,   the country
seen from the air.

LITTLE ENOUGH

On President Street a lady standing in her yard
reminded me of every aunt I ever met, stiff-backed
and tired but laughing in a rough loud voice.
'*You ever see such ugly furniture?*' Everything for
sale; a chest, table, counter and chairs, bent lamps
and broken cabinets. '*But the way things are, if it
stands still, I'd sell it.*' She laughed and I
could not leave, for hope she'd laugh again.
'*You girls out walking on such a pretty day,
why don't you just buy me out and let me go in?
You look at this stuff. This an't bad stuff.
Ugly but strong like they say, and clean, clean.*'
Which it was – scrubbed up and polished, oiled shiny
in the sunlight, like that lady and her concrete yard.

'*You girls,*' she smiled at us, invited us in to
see her new kitchen, the furniture set aside,
the walls redone. '*I've lived here twenty years,
worked forty for the city. You got to work, you know
even when the body wants no part of it. You got to work.*'
I know. I have always known. I smiled at her and
memorized her address,   watched the light at her
temples, the tight hair lightening with age,
her hands swinging a spray bottle of polish and
a flat yellow cotton rag.   *I know.   I know.*
I praised her walls, her cabinets, hugged to myself
her forty years of stubborn work, survival.

The women I dream of loving take care of themselves,
their people, put up shelves in the evening,
boil off chicken stock before bed, sleep hard and

3

are up again before dawn for the quiet, the hope of
a few good lines, another little piece of a story.

Like her, that old woman on President Street, as sturdy
as her pine cabinets and hand-scraped doors.   '*You girls,*'
she said and I knew then why she'd stopped us, what
she'd seen in how Barbara touched my neck, knew that
none of us would say the word, say *lesbian* or even *lovers*.

We would talk instead of houses, kitchens and
furniture, and how it is, making your own way in a
world where nobody's handing out anything for free,
of soup recipes and bean dishes rescued from burning pots.
'*God ain't gonna reach down and smooth things,*' she laughed.
'*God's got enough on his mind.*' She waved her hand as if
to say god's got little enough to do with us.
'*But you can do it. Get yourself a piece of
something important to you and work it, work it
with time and effort and care.*' In the code
we were speaking, I could not tell if she meant
the house
or life
or love.

Jane Barnes

BLOOMING

I wish you could be here to see my amaryllis
bloom   the first bulb I ever grew   the
first plant I ever had with an exotic name
the kind you want to say   How am I supposed to
know what that is?   Right now it's just
this single fat green spear like one
asparagus   you remember those asparagus jokes
I'm sure   you'd probably say   get that little
boy weewee out of here and then I'd say back
so refined   but that's my amaryllis   soon to be
a big red trumpet   or do I mean strumpet
you know just like if I bought a femmy red
dress with ruffles   flashy and loud and then
the amaryllis blooms   I bloom and you bloom
coming back and lifting up my skirt just in time

HOW IT STARTS

Know how it starts? she leaves her
watch on your bedside table and you
leave a shirt at her house then
you wear a jacket of hers home in the
rain and she starts to keep a T shirt
in your bureau just in case then it's
two toothbrushes and backup wheat germ
and kelp because she doesn't eat wheat
germ and you don't eat kelp and then
you make a corner for some of her
things and you begin to think of the
end of her couch as your end of the
couch and after that you might as well
just throw in the towel

I WANT YOU

I want you
to be good

for a few
poems

I want you
to be bad

for a good
many more

I want you
to be

beyond
poetry

I hardly
ever get there

with anyone

NO
for Linda

sometimes when I stop   you hot
dead cold it is because I learned
so early a lover was a man   a lover
was a wanting one   you had to give him
what he wanted   and wanting in me dies

sometimes when I stop you   dead
it is because I see his   need so big
yawning back at me from bad dreams bad
memories so hard   I never want to
touch   be touched   again

o love   it is not you   I fear
I do not say no   to you but to
all those times I turned toward him to
touch you   and you were not there
not here   no

HOMOPHOBIA

When I came out
to her   she started
calling me
you people

Judith Barrington

NAMING THE WAVES

We are done with feeling all the same —
done with that blind joy
of sudden recognition:
womanness alone will not get us through.

Our differences are like the oceans —
all bodies of water, yes
but take me, eyes bound, to any shore;
remove the blindfold and I recognize the sea.

Atlantic grey is not
Pacific green-grey is not
Aegean clear-green, though we hardly know
the words to describe the differences.

There are places, though
where patterns in the water
guiding sailors
have names in certain languages.

PASSING

Light-fingered wind teases our bare skin
as we stride with an easy rhythm

for two good miles, breasting the hill
in shorts, socks and dusty boots

between salmon-pink ponderosas
crusty bark, etched with black.

At an unexpected bend in the trail
we stop, face to face with strangers –

the woman in front, shielding him
from our bare breasts and clumsiness.

In the blazing sun, the red bandanna
drags over my eyes, the hasty shirt

catches my sunglasses; I blush;
I curse, needing to pass.

The shirtless man mumbles
close to me on the foot-wide trail

and I cover my sweaty breasts –
blushing and cursing and passing.

LESBIAN

Nobody said *the word*
when school dismissed two girls
who lay in the long grass hand in hand.
Friends sniggered

said things I couldn't hear
but I strolled across the muddy field
as if by chance
watching the long grass
from the corners of my eyes.

I did not think *the word*
as her hand moved mine to her breast
and she became my first lover.
The word waited, stranger than death,
while we touched each other's bodies.
Later I blamed her, thinking I was sick:
'I was so young' I said
'You took advantage of me'
but we never said *the word* and she drank each day.

The first time I heard it said aloud
my sister and her friend
were talking P.E. teachers
and I had already loved three women.
My stomach tipped; stopped breathing;
hot pools of blood flooded my face.
It was springtime; there was a weeping willow
and daffodils and this word
bumping around in the landscape.

Linda Bean 🖋

A WISH

I'd like you to meet my mum.

She'd cook us
a nice dinner
roast or chops for a guest.
You settled in front of the tele
me busy with drinks
and table laying.
We'd do it properly too
pull out the table
no trays for you.

Then we'd eat – noses in the tele

which i never seem to watch these days
plates piled high
– potatoes, meat, loads of gravy
'And there's plenty more outside!'
And pudding – ice cream and tinned fruit
or maybe apples and custard
we never were a dessert sort of family.

Yes, we'd eat
bellies full and fat
rolling into armchairs.
I'd make tea
– with persuasion
when we'd sit down
– you know just chatting.

Later,
you'd go to the loo
and mum would whisper
in the kitchen
between dishes
'She's very nice and so down to earth – ordinary'
And i couldn't help but agree.

Robin Becker

THE SCULPTOR HEARS THE SMALL BIRDS

In the studio, you are working
on love, wrapping
the fibers loosely
around the body, singing
with the radio like the women
of Madagascar, winding
raffia for baskets and hats

praising their supple hands.
Wild roses coil
about the barn, tight
as an embrace. A good idea
becomes a stand of fir trees
or a flock of small birds momentarily
filling the sky with wings.

You hear them rising
on the columns of warm air
as they pass from your life –
reconciling change
with the longing
to be still. Meanwhile, the piece
is pulling you back

to childhood
fears of beaks and talons and feathers
and bodies swelling
with desire. Like a figure seen
through dense branches
a shape begins
to sing in your fingers

first a red song
and then a white
song and then the steady
winter song of the sun
grazing the fields of snow.

A GOOD EDUCATION

First, there's daddy, big spender, picking up
the check & mother glancing into his fist
trying to see. She notes the tags
hanging from the dresses, but in the men's
store, he says *one of these & two of those*
without looking.
    It wasn't fair, who got
what & why. I never knew what anything cost
until it was *too much* or *cheaply made* or *not for us*.
Fractions I never got either, subtracting pieces
from pieces of things. When it was pies, OK,
but when it was point zero zero four,
I ended up weeping.
     Geometry was the last straw;
they let me out & shipped me up to Latin –
matching the subject with the verb ending,
searching for the missing preposition.
Latin was like long division: once you memorized
the tables, you kept dividing & dividing until

the row was done. On & on the numbers fell
like a connect-the-dots game. As long as you knew
the multiplication tables, the numbers
came out perfectly divided.
                          Next came word problems,
questions of ladders & shadows & the sides of houses.
How did you get the little phrase right up next
to the word it modified, so that you didn't have
the farmhouse marching through the grass but the farmer?
You had to scoot the unnecessary parts up close
to the necessary man sweating through the fields.
                          Every week,
there were at least six new things every day.
Who would keep up? Laura & Anne & Penny Sharp
were neck and neck; I was the class clown, in the middle,
thank God not at the bottom like Betsy & Suzanne,
The periods were fifty minutes; if it was your good subject,
you wanted it to last; if it was your bad, you tried,
you tried to understand what she was writing on the board,
but you were wishing that someone would throw up,
or there would be a fire drill, or like the day when
      Kennedy died,
everyone had to go home with her mother.

WHEN FRIENDS LEAVE
for Brad Crenshaw and Debra Gorlin

Breakfast is no fun
                    Boots are silent
No one bangs his head   No one falls
                          laughing in the snow
When friends leave   snow flies horizontal
The dog cries at the door
                    every chair is irritable
The wooden bowl waits upside down
                    coats are hung on hooks in the hall
We do not talk about the oak pegs
                    and the house of hewn logs
Brad does not pretend to be the itinerant thatcher
                    come to mend the roof
and we wish   stopping to have a few words with the farmer
that he was here to see the cows hunker against the barn

11

We sit close   near the stove   feel their shadows
pass behind us reaching for books   We do not pretend
            to live in Holland
                under the same roof
                with animals and fodder
When they were here   we found shingles of elm bark
trails through birch meadows   a silo with a cupola
Now we remember the patient eyes of Debra   beautiful
            listening   and the happy arrangement
of stones in their courses   lacing a path through the field

ON NOT BEING ABLE TO IMAGINE THE FUTURE

Picture the house,
the furniture, the cat,
or you may never have them.
In order to possess
you must envision.
If you fail to imagine your lover
you won't recognize her on the street
when opportunity presents itself
like a bill in the grass.
If you're nearing thirty
practice feeling forty or fifty.
If you don't train
you'll never learn
to play the violin or grow old.
Time will pass
but you won't be able to retire
or plan ahead
because you never planned ahead.
There will be no summer house,
no lake in New Hampshire,
no packing up the car,
no beautiful small children.
A trunk slams,
everyone piles in,
this is someone else's life.

Beth Brant

HER NAME IS HELEN

Her name is Helen.
She came from Washington State twenty years ago through
broken routes
of Hollywood, California,
Gallup, New Mexico,
Las Vegas, Nevada,
ended up in Detroit, Michigan where she lives in #413
in the gut of the city.
She worked in a factory for ten years, six months, making
carburettors for Cadillacs.
She loved factory work.
She made good money, took vacations to New Orleans.
'A real party town.'

She wears a cowboy hat with pretty feathers.
Can't wear cowboy boots because of the arthritis
that twists her feet.
She wears beige vinyl wedgies. In the winter she pulls on
heavy socks to protect her bent toes from the slush and rain.

Helen takes pictures of herself.

Every time she passes those Polaroid booths,
one picture for a dollar,
she closes the curtain and the camera flashes.

When she was laid off from the factory
she got a job in a bar, serving up shots and beer.
Instead of tips, she gets presents from her customers.
Little wooden statues of Indians in headdress.
Naked pictures of squaws with braided hair.
Feather roach clips in fuschia and chartreuse.
Everybody loves Helen.
She's such a good guy. An honest-to-god Indian.

Helen doesn't kiss.
She allows her body to be held when she's had enough
vodkas and Lite beer.
She's had lots of girlfriends.
White women who wanted to take care of her,

13

who liked Indians,
who think she's a tragedy.

Helen takes pictures of herself.

She has a picture on a keychain, along with a baby's shoe
and a feathered roach clip.
She wears her keys on a leather belt.
Helen sounds like a chime, moving behind the bar.

Her girlfriends took care of her.
Told her what to wear
what to say
how to act more like an Indian.
'You should be proud of your Indian heritage.
Wear more jewelry.
Go to the Indian Center.'

Helen doesn't talk much.
Except when she's had enough
vodkas and Lite beer.
Then she talks about home,
about her mom,
about the boarding schools,
the foster homes,
about wanting to go back to see her people
before she dies.
Helen says she's going to die when she's fifty.

She's forty-two now.
Eight years to go.

Helen doesn't kiss.
Doesn't talk much.
Takes pictures of herself.

She touches women who are white.
She is touched by their hands.

Helen can't imagine that she is beautiful.
That her skin is warm
like redwood and fire.
That her thick black hair moves like a current.
That her large body speaks in languages stolen from her.
That her mouth is wide and full and when she smiles
people catch their breath.

'I'm a gay Indian girl.
A dumb Indian.
A fat, ugly squaw.'
This is what Helen says.

She wears a t-shirt with the legend
Detroit
splashed in glitter across her large breasts.
Her breasts that white women have sucked
and molded to fit their mouths.

Helen can't imagine that there are women
who see her.
That there are women
who want to taste her breath and salt.
Who want a speech to be created between their tongues.
Who want to go deep inside her
touch places that are dark, wet,
muscle and spirit.
Who want to swell, expand two bodies into a word
of our own making.

Helen can't imagine that she is beautiful.

She doesn't kiss.
Doesn't talk much.
Takes pictures of herself so she will know she is there.

Takes pictures of herself to prove she is alive.

Helen takes pictures of herself.

Lorraine Bray

NOT 'OUT' TO GET HER

Sat behind a woman on the bus,
Didn't like the way she clutched her purse.

She smelled of something rich,
Of 'Cherry Lips',
She smelled of warm things, smelled sweet,
Of summer afternoons or rotting meat.
That woman wouldn't thank me,
Wouldn't take it kindly,
If I called her anything but 'lady'.

15

Olga Broumas

LITTLE RED RIDING HOOD

I grow old, old
without you, Mother, landscape
of my heart. No child, no daughter between my bones
has moved, and passed
out screaming, dressed in her mantle of blood

as I did
once through your pelvic scaffold, stretching it
like a wishbone, your tenderest skin
strung on its bow and tightened
against the pain. I slipped out like an arrow, but not before

the midwife
plunged to her wrist and guided
my baffled head to its first mark. High forceps
might, in that one instant, have accomplished
what you and that good woman failed
in all these years to do: cramp
me between the temples, hobble
my baby feet. Dressed in my red hood, howling, I went –

evading
the white-clad doctor and his fancy claims: microscope,
stethoscope, scalpel, all
the better to see with, to hear,
and to eat – straight from your hollowed basket
into the midwife's skirts. I grew up

good at evading, and when you said
'Stick to the road and forget the flowers, there's
wolves in those bushes, mind
where you got to go, mind
you get there,' I
minded. I kept

to the road, kept
the hood secret, kept what it sheathed more
secret still. I opened
it only at night, and with other women
who might be walking the same road to their own

16

grandma's house, each with her basket of gifts, her small hood
safe in the same part. I minded well. I have no daughter

to trace that road, back to your lap with my laden
basket of love. I'm growing
old, old
without you. Mother, landscape
of my heart, architect of my body, what other gesture
can I conceive

to make with it
that would reach you, alone
in your house and waiting, across this improbable forest
peopled with wolves and our lost, flower-gathering
sisters they feed on.

LANDSCAPE WITH NEXT OF KIN

Imagine father that you had a brother were
not an orphan singly that you had a twin
who moved away when he got married had
a kid a similar career whom you had not seen
but heard from frequently for thirty years
imagine meeting him some evening somewhere
familiar to you both not in the village but by
the sea/perhaps/you have

been talking for hours
and for many days
at ease in the proprietor's
gaze – he is young you are old he could have been
a soldier in your regiment that northern province
not so long ago/perhaps he is/you are

here this evening you and your brother seated at the damp
alloy table rusting in some seaside
Patra of the mind identical sighting
the prow of the ferry from Brindisi/perhaps/a woman

bows out from the throng
of tourists very feminine and very strong
resemblance to this man your brother you have never
married/yourself/tonight
are you sipping

17

the weak milk of your ouzo
having heard everything/at ease/on the other side
of the customs waiting for his daughter your
first blood kin is there anything
in the love you feel

swimming towards him as you did
nine months one heartbeat

pounding like an engine in those waters/is
there anything you won't forgive
her/him

Roz Calvert 🖋

WHITE TRASH GIRL

White trash girl
ain't you scared of me
like I'm scared of you?
Afraid we gonna blow our cover
gonna name each other
gonna wind up back
where we just bust outta
pluckin' turkeys, flippin' burgers
and waitin'

Ain't I afraid you're gonna
look too close, remember me,
and see . . . there ain't no
bank account, resume, insurance plan
no plan at all
and I'm still walkin' around soft
on the edge of the carpet

Powdered-milk face girl
I seen you
gettin offa the greyhound bus
back then, the same day I did
But I was sure
that you and me
was goin' different places.

18

Ain't it funny
do you recall
hillbilly, hick, greaser girl,
when yer mama gave mine
her Friday tips
so my sister could
go to the doctor
And nobody told
nobody's papa?

Red-fox eyed girl
I seen you too, at the parties
and po-lit-ical affairs
over-admirin' your own new shoes
goin' for the beer
when they start to talk
about root canal and school vacations.

Ain't it funny
do you recall,
hillbilly, hick, greaser girl,
when yer folks said mine was
that trash up the hill
and my folks said yer's was
that trash down the road?

White trash girl
ain't you scared of me
like I'm scared of you
Afraid we gonna rock the boat
if we start to talk
about pov-er-ty
and corn meal mush
in the middle
of the fem-in-ist
rev-o-lu-shun?

Shun, shun
you never been my lover
Shun, shun
never ate no bread
nor beans together
Shun shame
never killed no pain together

19

White trash girl
did you ever think
you'd choke on that
country silence?

Shun shame
call my name
Hillbilly, hick, linthead girl
Hillbilly, hick, greaser girl
My mama said false pride
that ain't no pride at all
Shun shame
call my name
Hillbilly, hick,
White trash girl

GET OVER

She watched closely
the hole in her pocket
so the world would not fall out
She walked around
Who knew
Who could know
she had the world in her pocket
Squeezed it in her warm hand
saying . . . Someday
not now
gotta hide it
so no one think I stole it
But someday
I get down the street
around the corner
lemme take it out
lemme have a looksee
She watched closely
the hole in her pocket
she watched her back
she watched her step
Lightfooted down the street
around the corner
And no one ever knew

MARILYN

A woman from the factory
moved in at the farm with her
after he moved out.

Some of the folks
said it was because
she was afraid
to be there alone
without my cousin
who was her husband
who moved out.

She never looked afraid
of anything to me.

Other folks said
in quieter tones
that she was livin'
with the one from the factory
like a woman lives with a man.

They would drive home fast
smokin' cigarettes together
after the three to eleven
in a jacked up chivy.

They'd wake the kids up
to say goodnight
in tight blue jeans
smellin' like grain and sweat together
let the dogs out together
fall into bed like a woman and a man . . .
like a woman and a woman
like two women.

They would dream asleep
like two women . . .
working in a factory
living on a farm
raising kids and dogs and hell together

They would dream asleep
like two women living
like they were not afraid.

CRACK CORN

Jimmy Crack Corn and
I don't care Jimmy Crack Corn
I don't care if they say my Mama
never slept that soundly.
Jimmy Crack Corn and
I don't care if they say my folks
lived twelve in four rooms.
Jimmy Crack Corn and
I don't care Jimmy Crack Corn
I don't care if they say my Mama
turned her eyes away.
I was pretendin' I was pretendin'
I was makin' believe
that she looked out for me.
I said she never knew and
I said it over and over
by way of pretendin' that no one knew,
just me and that whisker face
Daddy bad Daddy who
been hittin' on me since
I been three and four,
since I been five and six
and she never knew
I told me over and over
by way of makin' believe.

Step on a crack
break your mother's back.
Step in a hole
break the sugar bowl.
Fly's in the sugar bowl
shoo fly shoo.
Fly's in the sugar bowl
if Mama knew, she'd
kill that Daddy bad Daddy
put the papers out on him.
Get a big daddy swatter
come hell or high water
my Mama would stick
by me blood's thicker than water.
By way of makin' believe.
Cross my heart and hope to die

stick a needle in my eye
Mama don't know
fly's in the sugar bowl
shoo fly shoo
fly's in the sugar bowl
shoo fly shoo fly
bad fly Daddy
sticky, sicky Daddy
only tastin' my sugar
cause Mama don't know
and Mama don't know
cause I pretend she don't know
else she'd kill that
double crosser Daddy bad Daddy
and die of a heart got broke.
I was pretendin' I was pretendin'
I was makin' believe
cross my heart and hope to die
stick a needle in my eye
Mama don't know.
Mama don't know
but only because I'm makin' believe
Jimmy Crack Corn and
I don't care Jimmy Crack Corn.
Don't you see Jimmy Crack Corn?
Step on a crack
break your mother's back.
Step in a hole
break the sugar bowl.

WALDORF ASTORIA

Hazel who dusts away
the dust daily
in places where
white people
rich people
sit and collect

Hazel with a bad
toe yelling out
loud in her shoe

is talking to herself
outlouder every year

And the halls get
longer between
the rooms and the rags get
dirtier faster
the dust gets
thicker up her nose
down her lungs
and Hazel is
arguing louder
with her hobblin
toe every year.

Chaucer Cameron

THE RECIPE

Janice picks a microscopic particle and in her juvenile brilliance pieces together the reminiscent fragments of her delusions. To begin the renovation of disaster, you need the basic Recipe.

RECIPE
You must remember to gather all the ingredients together into one place. You need 500 grams of feeling,
    1 sieveful of sensitivity,
    20 grams of undercurrent insecurity,
    1½ litres of warm optimism,
    and 1 kilo of Womanhood.
(Important to note: Do not forget the conditioning.)

Mix together the feeling and sensitivity, until it is a tearful runny consistency. Place by the window for about an hour, then slowly add the insecurity bit by bit and stir well until it becomes firm to the touch. Leave in a heated room preferably near a warm record-player, volume 1 for a day and a half, or better still, leave over the weekend to rise.

To Decorate:
You need 1 kilo of the Male sex, making sure that it has been deep frozen to at least 10 degrees below zero, 5 degrees lower than the average man. Make sure that it is cold enough to counteract the

warmth of the ingredients shown above, otherwise the two will mix together before time.
You need precisely half a litre of bitter verbal,
    one cupful of extreme insincerity,
    and two packets of physical power.

The preference for decorating it in the kitchen or the bedroom is entirely up to the individual's own tastes.

Pour in the half litre of bitter verbal,
    the one cupful of extreme insincerity,
    carefully open the packets of physical power,
and mix together until the ingredients swell,
and become almost solid.
Finish off with a sprinkling of scathing remarks
and punch into shape.
Carve into the shape of a superficial relationship
and paste on.
Put into a hot oven, for what I call the honeymoon period,
which is precisely one hour.
Then test.

When ready check that the edges are slightly burnt, and that the frayed nerves which have risen to the surface are properly shattered.
This is a good sign that the mixture has blended well.
It should be left to mature overnight, if cut too early it will
be hard and unresponsive (a sign that the bitter verbal has come in contact with the insecurity).
Stab with the sharp point of a knife, and if the point is covered in crimson it will then be ready.
Cut into nine individual slices, within fifteen minutes of consuming, one will pass out in a delicate fashion for the rest of the year.

After regaining consciousness, one should remember never to attempt the Recipe again.

Andrea R. Canaan

GIRLFRIENDS

You know, the kind of woman friend you
can be a girl with.
You know what I mean a woman you giggle

with one minute and can be dead serious
the next.
The kind of friend that you can be a bitch
with and she thinks that you were being
a bitch just then, and tells you so.
The kind of friend that you usually
tell all to and when you forget to tell
her some secret that you have been holding
and casually mention it to her, you are
surprised that you hadn't told her.
You know, the kind of friend that you can
go out with and it's not always dutch.
The kind of woman friend that you
play with and sleep with and go to
the movies with and gossip half the day
or night with and argue politics with and
never agree yet always agree with . . . you know?
The kind of friend that you keep secrets
for and with and can be P.I. with, in fact
you both insist upon it.
I mean the kind of friend that you laugh
and cry with over some woman breaking your
heart even though this is the fourth time
this year it's happened, and she will hold
you and let you wail
just like it was the very first time your
heart was ever broken.
The kind of woman that will leave
no stone unturned to find out why she hurt
your feelings even if she didn't mean to and
especially if she did.
The kind of friend that you will accept
an apology from graciously even when you feel
now that you might have been being hyper-
sensitive that day and revel in the knowing
that someone cares so much how you feel and
you don't have to worry about monogamy or
polygamy or which side of the bed is yours
or nothing.
The kind of woman friend that you can tell
how your lover done you so wrong and she
doesn't get mad when you don't do all those
things you swore you would.

The kind of friend that you can get
mad with or strongly disagree with or lose
it with and she will not give up on you
or stop loving you.
The kind of friend that will give
you space to fall in love even though your
new affair is taking the spontaneity out
of her being able to pop over or to
call you late about some small bit of
info to hear your voice and be assured
about some fear that you can not
yet name.
The kind of friend that doesn't get mad
until she has not seen or heard from you
for two solid weeks and then she comes
over or calls and cusses your ass out for days
and then you go out for an ice cream cone.
I mean the kind of friend that stays mad
with the people that fuck over you long
after you have forgiven them.
The kind of friend that
allows you to wallow in self pity for
just so long and then gives you a swift
kick.
The kind of friend that close or far apart
she will be there for you, the distance wiped
away instantly to meet some outside enemy or
trouble.
I mean the kind of woman who always honors
what is private and vulnerable for you.

You know, I mean girlfriends.

Chrystos 🖋

ONE FOOL TO ANOTHER
for Bonnie Price

   When the owls called to us we rode through a breaking
dawn sky beadwork patterns racing between our hands
   Our fingers spoke when the small birds sang so sweetly
closing our long night of stones   words   memories
   women in common

You entered with a soft feet spirit
We called to one another in voices of owls
We called to one another in morning songs
   I heard the tree branch shake a bouquet of snow to the ground
                  both of us far from home
We rode to where I live   to the Three Sisters Mountains   to
   deep
green hills where you live   to stones we leave behind
   We called to the owls from our horses
   We called to the snow
            to the indigo sky
We were so beautiful everybody thought
         the sun was rising

Jan Clausen

SESTINA, WINCHELL'S DONUT HOUSE

Watching the black hours through to morning
I'd set out each successive tray of grease-
cooked donuts on the rack, chocolate and pink-
frosted, to harden beneath the fluorescent light,
talk to crazy Harry, count the change,
listen to top-forty radio. Mostly, I was alone.

Every stranger's suspect when you're alone.
A woman was beaten badly early one morning
by a man who sneaked in the back while she made change,
so I'd rehearse scenarios of scooping grease,
flinging it at the assailant's face, cooking the light
or dark flesh to curl away at the impact, angry pink.

The cab drivers came in every night, faces polished pink
and boyish, arriving in pairs or alone.
Their cabs clotted like moths at the building's light.
They were outlaws and brothers, despised men who rise in the
   morning.
They'd swagger, still dapper, if fattened on sweets and grease,
call me sugar and honey. I smiled. I kept the change.

Often I was too busy to see the darkness change,
flush from black to blue to early pink.
At four o'clock, my face smeared with congealed grease,

I think I was happiest, although most alone.
The harder hours were those of fullblown morning,
fighting depression, sleeping alone in the light.

Linda came in at six, awash with light,
businesslike, making sure there'd be enough change
to get her through the rigors of the morning.
She had a hundred uniforms; I remember pink.
Sometimes she'd cheat, leave me to work alone,
sneak out to flirt in parked cars, fleeing lifetimes of grease.

I can see her cranking the hopper, measuring grease,
indefatigable, wired on coffee, just stopping to light
her cigarettes. She didn't want to be alone.
It was only my fantasy that she could change,
stop wearing that silly, becoming pink,
burn free of the accidents, husband and children, some morning.

I remember walking home those mornings, smelling of grease,
amazed in summer's most delicate pink early light,
to shower, change, and sleep out the hot day alone.

APOSTATE

'But revolutionary poetry becomes weak
when it begins to extol the longed-for
future as already realized, or in the
process of realization . . .'
Czeslaw Milosz

Furthermore, I abjure
these textile metaphors.

I discover I do not choose
to sew spin weave quilt
mend knit darn braid
appliqué tat or crochet
my way through
a whole new
distaff poetry;
fold the laundry
of uplift,
whiter than white,
into drawers.

I like to think of
Penelope the Greek
each night unpicking
her virtuous handiwork;

and when
I hear the word *nurture*
I reach for my
pen.

Caroline Claxton 🖋

LESBIAN

YOUR IMAGE:
I am a lesbian
I open cans with my teeth.
I have a domineering mother,
except when I have a domineering father,
sister, brother, school-friend, neighbour, gay man who came to
    read the gas meter
when I was six.
I creep out
at the dead of night
to steal men's underpants
which I wear – under my tweed skirt.
I live at Greenham
except when I live next door to you.
I go to drop-in centres
for left-wing-commie-cigar-smoking-butch-bulldykes-against-
    the-bomb
paid for by the GLC.
I have fourteen fingers
we grow extra ones
you know.
I leap out from under 'man'hole covers
to grab 'straight' women
And I'm secretly plotting with Russia
to 'dis-arm' Ronald Reagan.

HOW IT IS:
You've never quite got it right
about me
So let me tell you about myself.

I am complicated but
surprisingly average.
I do everything
and as for jobs:
I have a good job, a bad job, no job
I'm fired from jobs, I create jobs
I've worked just about any kind of job you can think of
except Prime Minister
unfortunately.

I am a thousand colours
and come from a thousand places
I come in a thousand places
and out in a thousand places.

I am behind you in the bus queue,
the cinema, the supermarket.
I live everywhere
except Buckingham Palace
as far as I know.

I am older than spoken word
traces of my bones lie in the stones
beneath your feet.
I am made of rock
harder than diamond
It cuts through your conventions
and your sticky, sticky lies.

I am more women than you would believe
And more woman than you would understand.

What am I?

Janna Davis

THE REFUGE

It's bloody hard, she said,
this noise and confusion,
me and the kids like sardines
jam-packed into this room,
more like a cupboard.
And when we first came,

not even knowing
what town we were in,
or even caring, except
we were away and safe
and together.
Then trying to cope,
to make sense of it all,
the social, housing and
all the legal stuff
scaring the shit out of me
in case he finds out
where we are.
But the amazing thing, she said,
is I slept last night,
really slept all through first time,
and couldn't believe it
in the morning.
It's the relief of knowing
he can't reach me, wake me,
hitting and punching
until he gets what he wants.
I feel like I'm healing
outside and in,
and I'm beginning to remember
who I am.

Mary Dorcey

DRUNKEN TRUTHS

She returned,
talking of a new peace —
a life gathered and full,
stripped of the old refuges
of sober lies and drunken truths.
Quiet in the country nights
fasting on poetry and brown rice,
she shares a bed of chastened love
where spiritual subtleties
have replaced the old
crude language of the flesh.

A community of loving couples,
they build together, against
harsh New England winters
one friend, it seems, still talks too much
and has not yet found her sister
but all things ripen
with time and labour.
She talked to us with earnest eyes
straining through grey smoke
– she would quit for sure
next week, she said –

But meantime she lit each cigarette
from the last and stored the pack
deep in a breast pocket.
As her pale lips grew tight about
each word in praise of work and abstinence
– tired but polite,
three hours before midnight,
I remembered an old and younger friend –
holding a room in the spell of her talk,
a lover in one arm, a bottle in the other –
drunk at dawn . . . and laughing.

IN THE CITY OF BOSTON

I have seen mad women in my time,
I have seen them waiting row on row,
I have seen the stripped flesh,
the abandoned eye,
I have seen the frothing mouth
and heard the cries,
I have seen mad women in my time
– I have never seen them mad enough.

In the city of Boston I once saw a woman
and she was mad – as mad as they come
(and oh do they come, mad women,
as often as the rest?)
She walked the street in broad daylight,
neat as a pin – a lady no doubt
in blue coat, blue hat, blue purse
blue shoes – the only note

out of place in it all
was her face – the peculiar angle
of her head; thrown back, jaws wide
and a scream so shrill poured out
it lifted the birds from her feet.

Sunshine in an elegant Boston square
choc-o-bloc with the office lot
loosed to eat,
no one turned, no one stared
from their clean cut day,
nobody cared to embarrass the mad.
She strode through that crowd
sealed right in her mind,
chin high, clutching her bag,
her terrible siren full on.

Mechanical agony guiding her step
until she reached the pavement's edge.
There at the crossroads
– an extraordinary thing –
her polished shoes halted,
she lowered her head,
the animal howl died in her throat –
stock still, patient, ordered
she stood
because the traffic light was red.

I have seen mad women in my time,
I have seen them burn
the skin from their breasts,
I have seen them claw a lover's eyes,
I have seen the blade across the bone,
have seen the frothing mouth
and heard the moan –
I have seen the abandoned faces
row on row,
I have seen mad women in my time
– I have never seen us mad enough.

NIGHT

I remember your neck, its strength
and the sweetness of the skin at your throat.

I remember your hair, long, in our way
drawing it back from my mouth.
How my hands slid the low plain of your back
thrown by the sudden flaunt of your loins.
I remember your voice,
the first low break
and at last the long flight
loosing us to darkness.
And your lips along my shoulder,
more sure, even than i had imagined,
how i guarded their track.

I ask you then
what am i to do with all these memories
heavy and full?
Hold them, quiet, between my two hands,
as i would if i could again
your hard breasts?

AMERICA

They had boasted it
as something special, an ancient house
in the European style.
As I entered the old rooms and felt
their years cluster about me
I was at peace for the first time.
I gazed out the dark windows, sheltered
by the knowledge that I was just one
of so many others, to have watched these
great trees do battle with the wind

Or heard their leaves break and fall
in an autumn dusk.
And I understod then the loneliness
that I feel in this brash new country,
where everything is being done
as though never before.
Where there are no other presences
to keep me company,
no guiding hand in shadow at an open
door. No echo beneath our talk

35

Of those other inhabitants
— the half-seen face in the glass
— the sigh of their lost conversation,
reminding me that we are not alone
and need not struggle so anxiously
always to be first or last.
I miss those presences, quiet about me.
Here in this young country it seems
the air is too thin to fill lungs
grown rich with the breath of ghosts.

BLOOD RELATIONS

Leaving
she bends to kiss you
slowly on each cheek,
drawing closer to let slip
a few last words
in your foreign tongue
and i, discreet,
embarrassed to be the chosen
the one who stays,
lower my eyes and pretend indifference
granting her one last intimacy.

Can you blame me then
if i forget,
that it is only your mother
saying goodbye after morning coffee
whose eyes as they acknowledge mine
are brilliant with shamed jealousy.

Elana Dykewomon

I HAD A DREAM . . .

I had a dream: I spilled a sack of salt in the road. No matter, my
friends said, we don't need salt.

But I remembered my grandmother sending me little burlap bags of
salt from Florida, and I said: that's the trouble with us. Salt is an

electrolyte, we need it to conduct electricity, the good feelings between us. No wonder we don't have the connections we need. We don't have enough salt.

In my dream, I decided then to call up every womon I could and tell them: you are the salt of the earth.

But when I woke I thought, damn, how am I going to do this, where am I going to find the time and the self-assurance to say, over and over again: you don't know me, but my dreams have given me the mission to spread my message: you are the salt of the earth.   It's an old message, but worth repeating.

I mean, how many time could I bear to have womyn hang up on me?

Then I remembered this anthology. What better place to start?

You are the salt of the earth. Pass it on.

EVEN MY EYES BECOME MOUTHS

Forgetting what I'm about
your naked belly appears to me
wet from the bath
as you walk around and I
am laying you down
with a palm on each of your sides
until full & pushed
you open
the pomegranate, the fig
got nothing on this as
I press my face
into the hot bowels of you
and even my eyes
become mouths
to drink that juice

U.A. Fanthorpe

GROWING UP

I wasn't good
At being a baby. Burrowed my way

Through the long yawn of infancy,
Masking by instinct how much I knew
Of the senior world, sabotaging
As far as I could, biding my time,
Biting my rattle, my brother (in private),
Shoplifting daintily into my pram.
Not a good baby,
No.

I wasn't good
At being a child. I missed
The innocent age. Children,
Being childish, were beneath me.
Adults I despised or distrusted. They
Would label my every disclosure
Precocious, naive, whatever it was.
I disdained definition, preferred to be surly.
Not a nice child,
No.

I wasn't good
At adolescence. There was a dance,
A catchy rhythm; I was out of step.
My body capered, nudging me
With hairy, fleshy growths and monthly outbursts,
To join the party. I tried to annul
The future, pretended I knew it already,
Was caught bloody-thighed, a criminal
Guilty of puberty.
Not a nice girl,
No.

(My hero, intransigent Emily,
Cauterized her own dog-mauled
Arm with a poker,
Struggled to die on her feet,
Never told anyone anything.)

I wasn't good
At growing up. Never learned
The natives' air of life. Conversation
Disintegrated as I touched it,
So I played mute, wormed along years,
Reciting the hard-learned arcane litany
Of cliché, my company passport.

Not a nice person,
No.

The gift remains
Masonic, dark. But age affords
A vocation even for wallflowers.
Called to be connoisseur, I collect,
Admire, the effortless bravura
Of other people's lives, proper and comely,
Treading the measure, shopping, chaffing,
Quarrelling, drinking, not knowing
How right they are, or how, like well-oiled bolts,
Swiftly and sweet, they slot into the grooves
Their ancestors smoothed out along the grain.

HALF-TERM

Always autumn, in my memory.
Butter ringing the drilled teashop crumpets;
Handmade chocolates, rich enough to choke you,
Brought in special smooth paper from Town.

(Back at school, the square tall piles
Of bread, featureless red jam in basins,
Grace, a shuffle of chairs, the separate table
For the visiting lacrosse team.)

Long awkward afternoons in hotel lounges,
Islanded in swollen armchairs, eyeing
Aristocratic horses in irrelevant magazines.
Should I be talking to Them?

(Back at school the raptly selfish
Snatch at self: the clashing
Determined duets in cold practising-
Rooms, the passionate solitary knitting.)

Inadequacies of presentation, perceived
By parents' temporary friends; hair, manners,
Clothes, have failed to adjust.
I don't know the rules of snooker.

(Back at school, the stiff reliable
Awkwardnesses of work. History test

On Monday morning. Deponent verbs.
I have never been good at maths.)

Saying goodbye. There are tears
And hugs, relief, regret. They,
Like me, return to a patterned life
Whose rules are easy. Unworthily

I shall miss chocolate, crumpets,
Comfort, but not the love I only
Sense as they go, waving to the end,
Vague in the streetlamps of November.

(Back at school the bullies,
Tyrants and lunatics are waiting.
I can deal with them.)

FATHER IN THE RAILWAY BUFFET

What are you doing here, ghost, among these urns,
These film-wrapped sandwiches and help-yourself biscuits,
Upright and grand, with your stick, hat and gloves,
Your breath of eau-de-cologne?

What have you to say to these head-scarfed tea-ladies,
For whom your expensive vowels are exotic as Japan?
Stay, ghost, in your proper haunts, the clubland smokerooms,
Where you know the waiters by name.

You have no place among these damp and nameless.
Why do you walk here? *I came to say goodbye.*
You were ashamed of me for being different.
It didn't matter.

You who never even learned to queue?

FROM THE THIRD STOREY
for Hazel Medd
'You have to be selfish to be a writer.'
'Monstrously selfish?'
'Monstrously selfish,' she said.
   Jean Rhys in David Plante's *Difficult Women*

Aunt Jane scribbles in the living-room.
When visitors come, she stuffs her work
Under the blotter, and joins in the chat.

(In the third storey, a curious
Laugh; distinct, formal, mirthless.)

Daughter Charlotte's first care is to discharge
Her household and filial duties. Only then
May she admit herself to her own bright sphere.

(There were days when she was quite silent;
Others when I could not account for
The sounds she made.)

Home duties are a small part of
The Reverend William's life. Reverently
Elizabeth, wife and mother, furnishes his study,
And writes in the dining-room,
Which has three doors.
(A vague murmur, peculiar
And lugubrious. Something
Gurgled and moaned.)

George is Agnes's husband. He and
Mistress Marian *what do people call her?*
Write in one room at their desks, drudging
To pay off his marriage's debts.

(A savage, a sharp, a shrilly sound.
The thing delivering such utterance must rest
Ere it repeat the effort. It came
Out of the third storey.)

Sister Virginia, childless wife,
Fathoms the metaphor of room.
But who is One? The upstairs lunatic –
Might she not be Oneself?

(A snarling, snatching sound,
Almost like a dog quarrelling.)

Between affairs, before marriages,
Jean (*I have called myself so many
Different names*) buys twelve technicoloured
Quill pens to cheer her bare table
In bedsit Fulham. And writes,

(She was standing, waving her arms,
Above the battlements, and shouting out
Till they could hear her a mile off.)

And sets the mad wife free to tell
Truth of mistress, divorcée, mother,
Aunt, daughter, sister, wife:

Now at last I know
Why I was brought here
And what I have to do.

Eve Featherstone

THERE WERE THREE IN THE BED
For Ellen, lots of love from Eve

There were 3 in the bed
And the little one said
That's my mother
My mother
That you're caressing in that unseemly way
Get on your bike and go away
Oh bother
Bother bother.

There were 3 in the bed
And the mother one said
Now darling
Sh darling
I love you both, but can't you see
That I need adult company
Like a lover
A lover.

There were 3 in the bed
And the lover one said
I can't stand it
can't stand it
I have been pinned to the wall for an hour or more
My foot's got cold hanging on the floor.
And now you're both listening I have more to say,
I won't get on my bike and go away
But motherhood was never my decision,
And take off that look of knowing derision.
I'm a woman with feelings too
And a lover with a child for me is new.

But one thing I know for sure,
3 in the bed and one hits the floor.
I don't know the answers and neither do you
So let's have a cuddle for 3 and not 2.

There were 3 in the bed
And they all said
Let's hug now, Let's hug now.

Paula Finn

POEM FROM SEARS, ROEBUCK AND COMPANY, BROOKLYN

1
'I'm still not satisfied
with the bathroom'
says the woman with the pink towels
on the checkout line
I notice the cotton tree
on the 36 dollar sheetset label means 60 percent
cotton/40 percent
polyester

2
over the phone
a friend says 'I used to think it was OK
to dress like you don't have money
if you don't have money
but I learned
if you need it
you better dress like you already got it'

3
the women on line
are planning what to buy
next weekend

4
Rosa goes out early
to get milk
white bread
cigarettes for her husband
33 degrees: her legs are bare

she is wearing sneakers and a raincoat
she does not leave the house if she doesn't have to
she keeps the right
amount of money in her pocket
she does not expect a giraffe
between her apartment and
the bodega/she is not waiting
for a kiss behind her ear
she does not require the full-
color collision
of the clouds
against the sky

5
Eulalia has
2 girls
a husband who beats her
1 couch
4 chairs
1 large bed
a pound and a half of rice
a pot of beans
1 can of tomato paste
2 onions
before
she runs out
of sugar she buys another bag
when her husband wants sex she has
sex/she expects
to pay at least once
for everything she gets
she buys 1 bottle of ketchup
no giraffe
a kiss could cost a lot

6
at Sears in Brooklyn
you could stay all day
on the second floor there is electric organ music
15 television sets
plants that don't need watering
in the basement
there is a woman talking into
a microphone/frying

eggs in a no-stick pan and
sliding them into the garbage

7
Eulalia does not leave her husband
and when you call me
alone
at night
and say 'I want to kill
myself'
I figure the work begins right here
the work begins
right here

Gudrun Fonfa

WELFARE WAS MY HUSBAND

11 yrs
longer than most marriages
we had a few falling outs
a little lying
cheating
running around

I played helpless
eyelashes fluttering
I felt helpless

Welfare was my old man
my unloving
head of household
absentee lord & master
my computer poppa

I got as much as most wives
got enough for toilet paper
used it as tissues
used it as napkins
used it as sanitary napkins

didn't need to dress up
didn't need to smile
my in-laws

were social workers
had to dress down
had to cry
had to

Welfare, welfare
we're not divorced
only separated
my daughter's not 18
you would take me back
you would provide for me
in the style
to which I've had to
become accustomed

I don't nag
I was a good wife
I never asked for
a clothing allowance
I never wasted medicaid
(couldn't face those Drs.)

I never went to welfare rights meetings
I knew my place
was at your side
I had no side

Welfare husband
he carries big stick
he can take away child
I was good & scared
I never got out of line
long lines

Do I miss your no face
your cheshire cat cock?
Do I miss your little
late checks?
Do I miss your hand-out
your punch in the face
the stomach?
Would I go back
as battered women do?

The safety of your impersonal
malevolent benevolence

Common law welfare husband
the whole country hates me
loves to take the pentagon
on shopping sprees
buy the bomb dress up clothes

while a country full
of welfare kids
window shop
at the salvation army
thrift shops

Welfare husband
flaunting
his mistress GM
Chrysler Lockheed
Grain farming Corporations
anyone could feed a family
of four on those table scraps

Promise me no surprises
no gift wrapped
have-a-heart animal traps
in the mail
no more forms to fill out

I said 'so long'
You said with a smirk
'write when you get work'

I'VE GOT THE GENERAL UNSPECIFIC – BLUES . . .

I've got the general
unspecific – no one's
left me – nothing's
wrong – Blues

the unexplained –
down in the dumps –
can't put my finger
on it – Blues

all pervasive
gloomy – moody

depression city
need a good laugh – Blues

my lover loves
me – nothing to complain
about – something's
sad/wrong – Blues

don't need a drink
the pot's homegrown
any old orgasm
will do – Blues

need a good cry
the house is too
calm – is my period
due – Blues

I've got the general
can't carry a tune
can't sing-a-long
no song – Blues

Jane Frances

WHAT I MEANT TO SAY

This place is not my home
But when I stayed away
We never met
So here I am
Pretending

               that where we are
               I am at home.

I fear that
I don't know
How to say
How to convey that

I'm a long way from home
Pulling my coat around me
To keep something in

               something out.

I come from another planet, you see,
Where everything's different
And I don't look away
From your eyes and your smile
And I touch your hair
And we kiss in the sun
And never need coats.

> I'm sorry
> I forgot
>   where we are.
> I meant to say
> Something dull
> And not quite true.

Sharon Franklet 🖋

KIKAMBALA MEMORIES/CHILDHOOD VACATION IN AFRICA

The lady was white.
The Black people did flips on cement.
We ate pineapple.

The lady wore a towel.
The Black people wore clothes.
I thought it would fall off.

She said she had run over a Black man.
Everybody clapped.
We ate ham, too, and swam in the ocean.

She wanted everything to go smoothly in court.
I was told that the Black people lived in the bushes near the beach.
Veiny bats hung sleeping over the pingpong tables.

Her blond hair was pulled tightly back.
Black people climb coconut trees like monkeys   they said.
After all, it had been dark.

Her eyes were dry.
The sea slugs on the reef scared me.

CUNT POEM

i like your cunt i said.
here i'll give her to you she said.
in a small mouthed drawstring bag made of course of silk/pink at that/
i carry now with me everywhere and wherever/her cunt. the silk gets
wet, drips sometimes a trail of imprints and odor and fluids from the
body.

in the pink silk sopping sometimes soundless sometimes wiggling
sighing shouting clingy drawstring bag i carry her. 'let me out' she
chants impatiently as i struggle with the knot at the top of the sack/
cursing, bending back nails.

or she runs to a corner and tries to be silent and unnoticeable, tries not
to seep thru the walls of silk, plays dead.

alone she leaps and twirls against the sides making billows and erup-
tions she whistles and hoorays/hollers and parades when i undo the
soft slippery stringed bow at the top and wink in; she causes frenzy
and envy.

in my pocket i can feel her warmth and wetness. the silk bag tied to my
beltloop, i wait for each step to bring her rocking and bumping back
into me, for the signs of aliveness, for desire.

like slithering fish the soft lips murmur in the darkness of the bag. i slip
fingers in to probe and stroke. they come out smelling and carry the
smell far into the day. it lodges firmly under short nails and announces
itself boldly to me in each movement with every shifting of the air. late
in the day the smell (even it seems the wetness has persisted under
the nails) climbs out, pries loose and wanders out upon boulders to
stretch in the sun, evaporate and mingle. left are only reminders and
souvenirs.

i push my whole hand in and grasp deeply, scraping down the sides of
the wet silk with my nails to make sure i leave nothing. or i use both
hands, holding the sack in my lap like a cat, running my hands down
its insides till they meet moist and pungent in the seepage at the
bottom. she feels like seagrasses massed together, like dying sodden
leaves, like oysters and mussels raw in the strainer before frying. i
move my hands through her, absorbing, eyes closed, caressing, letting
her take and suck my fingertips and run between the fingers licking
with smooth thick snaky tongues all the webbing between my fingers.
my blood and soul pour into my hands. i exist only in her thick
puddles, stroking and melting.

sometimes i dive in. all body. whole. or i climb in slow and push in with my shoulders, separating the deep firm lips and dragging my body down to nestle between them. i am held, tightly cradled between her lips. i must breathe carefully. the soft flaps lap at my shoulders and face. there is a dripping, it is cavernous in the faint faint light in the pink-silk darkness. i take off my clothes and slide and stretch along the length of her, scratch and tickle and pet and nibble her, grow calm and relaxed, grow waterlogged and replenished, grow sleepy and content.

DON'T STOP*
(villanelle for the bar; to be rapped)

monday's the day & you gotta dance
so find yr feet n put on yr pants
give it on up, yeah! and take the chance.

shoes clickglideslide they jump n prance
let yr body say what it's got/ta say
tuesday's the day & you gotta dance.

wednesday comes, you're in a trance
so move that body – shake off the day
say, give it on up and take the chance.

snap yr fingers   clap yr hands
let yr body say it   let yr body sway
thursday's the day & you gotta dance.

a wink a shake a wiggle enhance
the friday night search for the easy lay
so give it on up and take the chance.

saturday night and the girls are fancy;
y'walk on in an'   you're ready to play
today's the day & you gotta dance.

so what it's sunday, who sez ya can't?
let other folks stay home n pray
you give it on up and take the chance!
cuz today's the day & you gotta dance.

* *from a sugarhill gang rap song*

Kath Fraser

PRIVATE PUZZLES

Private puzzles she patterned on the sitting-room carpet:
'relationship', 'monogamy', 'jealousy', 'sexuality' –
dry words.
Just so much dust resting on the fibres.
Dust the colour of stale dreams and nightmares,
                    dull.
Knee-deep in dull dust she felt her left leg itch,
it would kick over the traces of old dreams.
She sat looking at fragments of
                    'relatio   ip'
                    ' exu   ity'
and sighed.
With the hoover she cleared an enormous space of colour
and invited a few friends to tea.

Jean Freer

HAIKU

And our fathers thought we were whores
        For in their fantasies
            They fucked us

Bea Gates

CONVERSATION WITH THE BODY

My sex opens like a fan: thigh, thigh, thigh –
bones like rays elongate; the breath

lights the fingers, the palms blink open
and listen to the air. The body swims
after it – out of breath.

No one is here beside me –
just the suspended questions

that shine – asking
how to touch. I hear
answering all along my spine. Stars
flex in the high hum of the dark.

I've broken out of expectations,
don't look for a lover
and yet, at first, inspect everything –
grumpy, kicking the newly empty
boxes around the rooms without
doors where the unexpected
moves ahead of me.

I'm talking now – taking my body
for a ride in the atmosphere   having
volcanoed out, spit rock from my stone lap,
violet-red pebble rage.
I inhabit the soft-hair surfaces,
hot-pulse the air
marking space like the tiger
in the tiger coat.

What is it, my hands could
almost touch? Open, unready,
not lost or waiting . . . this
body and no other.

SMALL WORLD
for Jean

I have no family, no small world
to step into. But the mouth of quarrels,
the shadows that go public, thoughts
loud as words.

I am here on my own
and lean towards wanting
to live under one roof like the one
we call day and let go night
shadowless.

This poem is for me and for all
of us. We are all
animals, fragile in this
small world.

I WRAP MYSELF

in the cellophane, clothes
just back from the dry cleaners –
twirl, enthralled inside
the bubbles. I join and separate
worlds, bunch up corners and trounce
them in an explosive pop,
breaking the film from the inside
out. My mother discovers me,
my held-in air, hand over
her mouth . . . *Never, never*
do that. You could suffocate.

This is the same room
where he handles me
as I seal off, let my skin
expand to take him in
and let myself out noiselessly
like bubbles breaking
away. You know the crazy dance
of escaping air, the object thrashing
into weightlessness. I am
the air, not the weight. I have
escaped, live outside every room
I enter.

Joan Gibbs

THE OTHER WOMAN

Being the other woman
sometimes ain't bad
especially when
you be the one
getting all the
best smiles, sweet
stolen hugs, surprise
flowers, kisses
that seem like
they'll never end.

Yes,
being the other woman
sometimes ain't bad
but when it isn't
it hurts
like Mama
trying to get
that straightening comb
through my hair
Saturday morning, afternoon, evening
didn't care whether
I cried, screamed,
called on God
let the neighbors
cross *and* down
the road know
that Phylis
was getting her hair done.

Janice Gould

THEY LOOK FOR THE DEEPEST GREEN

In the jungle
we look for the deepest green.
When our bodies steam,
humid, beaded with dark water,
we dream of fish,
translucent fins and tails,
infinitesimally small roe,
the journey upstream.
The fish hide
among gold waving weeds,
pulsing softly.
In pools they wait,
stunned by the river sound,
fearful to advance.
The jungle grows denser,
thick air beats against our skin,
and my reptilian brain
sees life uncoil in your womb,

life with amphibian force
turning sun and moon. We move
upstream, the pirogue tips
slowly upon churning water,
thick with salamanders.
Parrots scream above us,
blue-feathered and proud.
They open their ivory beaks
and beat their wings
against crumbling cliffs.
My shirt is unbuttoned,
your skin is wet.
Far off we hear air collide,
first with soft peals
which seem to roll the clouds together,
then with loud, white cracks,
fierce as the breaking of trees.
Suddenly the sky rains
frogs, bits of claw,
fish eggs,
muddy salt drops of water.
'Don't cry', I say,
but I do not know
which of us I mean.
Your hands fold
over your belly, hands
bone thin and sad.
If we travel further
upstream, to Inca ruins, far
above the furthest cascade,
from the high stone walls
we can look down
upon the verdant jungle
green as malachite or jade.
We will emerge into
pale violet light
and know
at our journey's source,
the fish remain hidden
in the cold, dark water.

WE EXIST

You write to me: 'Indians must be
the loneliest people on Earth.
Loneliness
              from our histories,
our losses,
even things we cannot name
                    which are inside us.
We write to counteract a history
that says we are a dead,
                 a conquered people.
It is like a shout in a blizzard.
We shout
          to prove we exist.'

In snow that December
At Wounded Knee, Sioux people
lay dead, dying
             their mouths frozen open.
Soldiers dug a ditch,
               dumped the bodies in.
Soil crumbled over them, then
their hearts fed on roots and stones,
their mouths filled with dust.

It is dawn,
The daughter lies on her bed,
legs drawn up,
her fist in her mouth.
I am poisoned, she thinks,
beneath my heart, I feel it.
This is what it means
              to be Indian.
My mother is not here.
They mined her
           for her grief,
they followed each vein,
invading every space,
removing, they said, the last
vestige of pain.
             At dawn,
this time of prayer,
the daughter,

in a voiced mined
                    from a sickness of soul,
tries to name,
                    to make words
which say
            we exist.

CAVES ON A MOUNTAIN

I
In late afternoon, at the edge
of a mountain, we observe light

falling across dry slopes of grass,
walls of black lava.

Today we are not in love
and our words take

the shape of crows. They fly
off in different directions.

II
Her hand has convinced her
I am here when

it rests on my neck,
and her cool fingers,

unsteady with desire,
twine in my hair.

III
Pointing above us she says,
there are caves up there

where Indians would go at night
seeking visions, listening for songs.

There are burn marks
where torches flared

against the rock ceiling.
Do you want to see?

I stare at damp earth,
the darkened leaves beneath us,

and answer, no.

THE CHILDREN WHO NEVER DEPARTED

In the long summer twilight
it may happen when the wind shakes
the aspen, the quake of leaves
awakens two children
buried on Cloud's Cap
above the Salcha River. They fly
straight up from their grave,
and the two souls wrap around
each other like a whirlwind.
Their laughter falls like shadows
on white stars of dogwood,
sends shivers through spruce,
into willows and birches along the river.
In the afternoon you may see them,
when picking mushrooms
you sweat to the crest of the bluff.
They stand quietly at the edge
of the glade, or lie clasping
one another amid moss and matted roots
in the damp, exploded earth.

Judy Grahn

THE COMMON WOMAN

(SELECTED VERSES)

I. Helen, at 9 a.m., at noon, at 5:15

Her ambition is to be more shiny
and metallic, black and purple as
a thief at midday; trying to make it
in a male form, she's become as
stiff as possible.
Wearing trim suits and spike heels,
she says 'bust' instead of breast;
somewhere underneath she
misses love and trust, but she feels
that spite and malice are the
prices of success. She doesn't realize
yet, that she's missed success, also,

so her smile is sometimes still
genuine. After a while she'll be a real
killer, bitter and more wily, better at
pitting the men against each other
and getting the other women fired.
She constantly conspires.
Her grief expresses itself in fits of fury
over details, details take the place of meaning,
money takes the place of life.
She believes that people are lice
who eat her, so she bites first; her
thirst increases year by year and by the time
the sheen has disappeared from her black hair,
and tension makes her features unmistakably
ugly, she'll go mad. No one in particular
will care. As anyone who's had her for a boss
will know
the common woman is as common
as the common crow.

II. Ella, in a square apron, along Highway 80

She's a copperheaded waitress,
tired and sharp-worded, she hides
her bad brown tooth behind a wicked
smile, and flicks her ass
out of habit, to fend off the pass
that passes for affection.
She keeps her mind the way men
keep a knife – keen to strip the game
down to her size. She has a thin spine,
swallows her eggs cold, and tells lies.
She slaps a wet rag at the truck drivers
if they should complain. She understands
the necessity for pain, turns away
the smaller tips, out of pride, and
keeps a flask under the counter. Once,
she shot a lover who misused her child.
Before she got out of jail, the courts had pounced
and given the child away. Like some isolated lake,
her flat blue eyes take care of their own stark
bottoms. Her hands are nervous, curled, ready
to scrape.

The common woman is as common
as a rattlesnake.

VII. Vera from my childhood

Solemnly swearing, to swear as an oath to you
who have somehow gotten to be a pale old woman;
swearing, as if an oath could be wrapped around
your shoulders
like a new coat:
For your 28 dollars a week and the bastard boss
you never let yourself hate;
and the work, all the work you did at home
where you never got paid;
For your mouth that got thinner and thinner
until it disappeared as if you had choked on it,
watching the hard liquor break your fine husband down
into a dead joke.
For the strange mole, like a third eye
right in the middle of your forehead;
for your religion which insisted that people
are beautiful golden birds and must be preserved;
for your persistent nerve
and plain white talk —
the common woman is as common
as good bread
as common as when you couldnt go on
but did.
For all the world we didnt know we held in common
all along
the common woman is as common as the best of bread
and will rise
and will become strong — I swear it to you
I swear it to you on my own head
I swear it to you on my common
woman's
head

A WOMAN IS TALKING TO DEATH

PART FOUR

A Mock Interrogation

Have you ever held hands with a woman?

Yes, many times — women about to deliver, women about to
have breasts removed, wombs removed, miscarriages, women
having epileptic fits, having asthma, cancer, women having
breast bone marrow sucked out of them by nervous or indifferent interns, women with heart condition, who were
vomiting, overdosed, depressed, drunk, lonely to the point
of extinction: women who had been run over, beaten up,
deserted, starved, women who had been bitten by rats; and
women who were happy, who were celebrating, who were
dancing with me in large circles or alone, women who were
climbing mountains or up and down walls, or trucks or roofs
and needed a boost up, or I did; women who simply wanted
to hold my hand because they liked me, some women who
wanted to hold my hand because they liked me better than
anyone.

These were many women?

Yes. many.

What about kissing? Have you kissed any women?

I have kissed many women.

When was the first woman you kissed with serious feeling?

The first woman ever I kissed was Josie, who I had loved at
such a distance for months. Josie was not only beautiful,
she was tough and handsome too. Josie had black hair and
white teeth and strong brown muscles. Then she dropped
out of school unexplained. When she came back she came
back for one day only, to finish the term, and there was a
child in her. She was all shame, pain, and defiance. Her eyes
were dark as the water under a bridge and no one would
talk to her, they laughed and threw things at her. In the
afternoon I walked across the front of the class and looked
deep into Josie's eyes and I picked up her chin with my
hand, because I loved her, because nothing like her trouble
would ever happen to me, because I hated it that she was
pregnant and unhappy, and an outcast. We were thirteen.

You didn't kiss her?

How does it feel to be thirteen and having a baby?

You didn't actually kiss her?

Not in fact.

You have kissed other women?

Yes, many, some of the finest women I know, I have kissed.
women who were lonely, women I didn't know and didn't
want to, but kissed because that was a way to say yes we are
still alive and loveable, though separate, women who recog-
nized a loneliness in me, women who were hurt, I confess to
kissing the top of a 55 year old woman's head in the snow in
boston, who was hurt more deeply than I have ever been
hurt, and I wanted her as a very few people have wanted
me – I wanted her and me to own and control and run the
city we lived in, to staff the hospital I knew would mistreat
her, to drive the transportation system that had betrayed
her, to patrol the streets controlling the men who would
murder or disfigure or disrupt us, not accidently with
machines, but on purpose, because we are not allowed out
on the street alone –

Have you ever committed any indecent acts with women?

Yes, many. I am guilty of allowing suicidal women to die
before my eyes or in my ears or under my hands because I
thought I could do nothing, I am guilty of leaving a prostitute who held a knife to my friend's throat to keep us from
leaving, because we would not sleep with her, we thought
she was old and fat and ugly; I am guilty of not loving her
who needed me; I regret all the women I have not slept with
or comforted, who pulled themselves away from me for lack
of something I had not the courage to fight for, for us, our
life, our planet, our city, our meat and potatoes, our love.
These are indecent acts, lacking courage, lacking a certain
fire behind the eyes, which is the symbol, the raised fist, the
sharing of resources, the resistance that tells death he will
starve for lack of the fat of us, our extra. Yes I have committed acts of indecency with women and most of them were
acts of omission. I regret them bitterly.

THE MEANINGS IN THE PATTERN

The interior of the Arizona Indian museum
is cool. A woman stands at the counter,
selling her family wares. 'I am a Pima,'
she says. 'We have always been here.
People say, where did the Anasazi go?
But we are right here, we never left.
We were farmers, always.
We were promised water for our gardens,
now they are taking it. My daughter
made the baskets; only girls are taught
to do it. My son made this pouch.'
She pats the small soft leather purse,
thick with close beading, red and white,
yellow and blue. The design: clouds,
a bird, a man, the earth.
'This picture tells a story,' she says.
Her black eyes looking inward and outward.
'No one who buys this could ever understand –
the meanings in the pattern. What it is
really worth.' Clouds. A
bird. A man. The earth. Her fingers
feel the beads. 'There is a story here.
It takes three days and nights to tell it.'

PARIS AND HELEN

He called her: golden dawn
She called him: the wind whistles

He called her: heart of the sky
She called him: message bringer

He called her: mother of pearl,
    barley woman, rice provider,
    millet basket, corn maid,
    flax princess, all-maker, weef

She called him: fawn, roebuck,
    stag, courage, thunderman,
    all-in-green, mountain strider,
    keeper of forests, my-love-rides

He called her: the tree is
She called him: bird dancing

He called her: who stands,
    has stood, will always stand
She called him: arriver

He called her: the heart and the womb
    are similar
She called him: arrow in my heart.

THE GOOD WEEF IS BOTH

The good weef is both
weaver and wife, those old
words meant the woman-as-a-maker,
not especially bonded
to one husband,
but to the Spider Woman of life,
the one with ties that bind,
knitter of the sacred, magic knots,
who with her scissors or her knife,
is tie-breaking life-taker,
queen of what-is-not.

Wife and weef and weaver,
she was the market-woman
of Europe. Ale-wife, she sold
the ale she brewed; oysterwife bawled
what from the mothersea she drew,
strawberrywife what she grew.

The fishwife brought her stinking
reputation with her to the modern ear,
reference, they say, to a certain smell,
said with a certain sneer. The smell is
of queens.

      The midwife stands midway
between the laboring weaver and her weaving
and the world, easing the way to life.
I am pleased to call myself a wife too,
a word-wyfe.

Pamela Gray

MRS RICHIE

A Richmond woman who has infuriated her neighbors by watering
her yard incessantly for more than a year was told by a municipal
court judge yesterday to turn off the water and keep it off.

East Bay Municipal Water District officials said Richie's water
usage was averaging 20,306 gallons a day. When told about the court
order, however, Richie increased her water use to 21,433 gallons
a day.

Asked why she keeps watering her property, Richie told a Tribune
reporter it was none of his business, cursed him and then walked
away, leaving the water still running.
– *The Oakland Tribune*, June 1984

mrs richie turned on her sprinklers
13 months ago
and refuses to turn them off.

she is turning richmond
into atlantis: water spills
over the edges of her
front lawn, onto sidewalks, over
curbs, into the street, water
shoots into the air, gushes
like oil, pours down her
front steps in a steady stream

the air is pungent
with algae and mildew,
the cement is crumbling,
the streets are muddy,
people halfway down the block
are slipping and falling

the neighbors are tired
of their soggy shoes, the muddy
paws of their dogs and cats
blotching their clean linoleum,
tired of living in this
wetness, the endless sound
of water like some biblical
rainstorm that just won't stop

mrs richie screams
through her screen door
    i ain't turnin
    off my water   i paid
    my bill   this water's
    mine

the white reporters snap pictures
of her angry black face,
smirk as they tell her story:
just another crazy black woman

what is it mrs richie
is watering   where
does she get $400 a month
for her water bills
what is it she wants
to cleanse   and why
is it taking so long

or is this just
the most power
mrs richie ever had
and she ain't ready
to turn if off

Caroline Griffin

CALL THIS A LIFE LIVED BACKWARDS

i
Call this a life lived backwards
this woman   I   am thirty-three
still inside my mother
she frowns as I reach out

                for anything.
She doesn't want me to go.
Will someone else hold her hand?
She is too young to have children
she is too young to be left alone
but it's choking me —
layers of mothers   have they swallowed
                each other?

It's too hot.
I would push out but she frowns too much
and her knuckles are tight.

ii
Divide 'I want' by 'I can'
    there's a lot of wanting left over
top-heavy   foolish   my legs can't carry this
    burden down the street.
Here is a label –
    I am agoraphobic
    and it's so hot
will no one hold my mother's hand?

and now two stones –
    'I am afraid to travel'
    'I am afraid to be on my own' –
these are cold stones
    use has rubbed off shame and anger.
I could not say this once.
Now I can provide a commentary
    it's a kind of splitting.

This is a life lived backwards –
    to want and then to ask
'what is possible'   this is division
    how can I love myself?
Wanting does not evaporate
    it goes on burning.
I try to kick it into shape
    kick it to understand
This is myself I talk about.

Yes I have felt
    a silence round my wanting
    a pause
the bruised mass speaks slowly
    it is too hard to keep on.
This is no way to live.

iii
Agoraphobia – I have shown consideration
for so long. I am polite – oh please don't
                                    leave me
politeness hides the smell of fear –

68

and patient   infinitely patient
it is a long indrawn breath.
I want it all back now.

iv
While this poem burns
my body stretches out.
I do not know the name of the sea
I do not try to know it.
I do not pass the waves through my hands
    hunting   what is this
I do not turn from my great strength
    to claw at this water
I do not ask if the sea is reliable.

I can rest on mysteries
my body stretches out upon them
the intense coiling inside me
listens   is here now.
You know some of my loving
in this there is a heavy turning strength
While the poem burns remember
I am the same woman.

TODAY IS FULL OF RAIN AND WIND

Today is full of rain and wind
the trees are showing the underside,
branches pushed too far back.
Today the bean-poles sway and I wonder
what holds, what catches,
remember the tight knots of sweet-peas
so light the wind can't tear them,
so light we can't be torn –

What holds, what catches?
The branches are pushed too far back.
Blake saw angels in the trees
I see my father, he is very small
and asking for some reason not to jump.
I give him a reason.

'By the Cross her station keeping
stands the Queen of Sorrows weeping' –

the road runs between Highgate and Golders Green
very straight, trees both sides. I see myself
standing there at risk to earth and sky –

The logs have been stored in a dry place.
They flare up now, efforts
towards an outcome beyond the power of our imagining,
visions, as though some being in magnificence emerged,
as though a lion roared in a corner of this quiet room –
and I see myself crying on the road
between Highgate Hill and Golders Green
crying out for you,
unable to be alone,
unable to put myself there.

Here is no glory.
I give away my pain. I burn my efforts
which might break through
into myself being alone.

I see angels everyday
they run off all the time anytime
leaving the everyday to me.
Blake saw angels in the trees.
I see my father, he wants to know why,
and I see a woman weeping in the road –
visions of suffering
towards an outcome beyond the power of my imagining.
I cry out for you – trying to hold on –
Is this in the nature of things?
None of us can bear it all the time.

Marilyn Hacker ✍

INHERITANCES

Iva asks me for stories of her father's
family. I learned them second-hand
– not even a Christian, and not black.
I think of a reflective membrane: classes,
mirrored, meld. She starts with slavery.
The eight-year-old hunkered in the old man's

barrel-staves to hide when the blue horseman
(she breathed in horse) leaned toward her grandfather
to shout, 'Old man, you're free!' While slavery
had slipped, a wristlet from the writing-hand
of the bisque-beige enrolled in Classes
for Young Ladies, in Paris, where her black

mother was not. Ledgers were in the black;
the permeated membrane not the man,
else childless, who exercised three classes'
prerogatives (landed, white, male) to father
twice the child who, by his power in hand,
was bred to, and released from, slavery.

Iva asks, 'Were your parents *for* slavery?
Were *they* slaves? I know they weren't black.'
She puts her suntanned hand against my hand,
compares. 'Does "manumit" mean, just a man
could make slaves free?' I tell her, my father
spoke German in his West Bronx first-grade classes;

my mother worked at Macy's, took night classes
at Hunter, read about Wage Slavery
and Profits in the kitchen, where her father
waited for her to make his breakfast. Black
dresses were required for work. A man
– Jewish, of course – would take her life in hand.

I don't wear any rings on my left hand.
Two copies of notes home from Iva's classes
are sent. Her father lives with a white man,
writes science-fiction novels: slavery
on far worlds, often, though the slaves aren't black.
She says, 'Dad's roommate,' or 'My other father.'

I wouldn't say to a black friend that class is
(in its erasures) slavery. I hand
down little to emancipate my father.

RUNE OF THE FINLAND WOMAN

for Sára Karig

'You are so wise,' the reindeer said, 'you can
bind the winds of the world in a single strand.'
H.C. Andersen, The Snow Queen

She could bind the world's winds in a single strand.
She could find the world's words in a singing wind.
She could lend a weird will to a mottled hand.
She could wind a willed word from a muddled mind.

She could wend the wild woods on a saddled hind.
She could sound a well-spring with a rowan wand.
She could bind the wolf's wounds in a swaddling-band.
She could bind a banned book in a silken skin.

She could spend a world war on invaded land.
She could pound the dry roots to a kind of bread.
She could feed a road gang on invented food.
She could find the spare parts of the severed dead.

She could find the stone limbs in a waste of sand.
She could stand the pit cold with a withered lung.
She could handle bad puns in the slang she learned.
She could dandle foundlings in their mother tongue.

She could plait a child's hair with a fishbone comb.
She could tend a coal fire in the Arctic wind.
She could mend an engine with a sewing-pin.
She could warm the dark feet of a dying man.

She could drink the stone soup from a doubtful well.
She could breathe the green stink of a trench latrine.
She could drink a queen's share of important wine.
She could think a few things she would never tell.

She could learn the hand code of the deaf-and-blind.
She could earn the iron keys of the frozen queen.
She could wander uphill with a drunken friend.
She could bind the world's winds in a single strand.

MOTHER II

No one is 'Woman' to another
woman, except her mother.

72

Her breasts were unmysterious
naked: limp, small. But I thought pus
must ooze from them: her underwear
like bandages. Blood came from where
I came from, stanched with pads between
her legs, under the girdle, seen
through gaping bathroom doors. Around
her waist, all sorts of rubber. Bound
to stop the milk, my milk, her breasts
stayed flat. I watched my round self, guessed
a future where I'd droop and leak.
But dry and cool against her cheek
I'd lean my cheek. I stroked the lace
and serge she sheathed her carapace
with: straight skirts, close cuffs, full sleeves;
was, wordless, catechized; believed:
nude, she was gaunt; dressed, she was slim;
nude, she was flabby; dressed, her firm
body matched her brisk, precise
mid-continental teacher's voice,
which she had molded, dry, perfect-
ed from a swamp of dialect.
Naked or clad, for me, she wore
her gender, perpetual *chador*,
her individual complex
history curtained off by sex.
Child, I determined that I would
not be subsumed in womanhood.
Whatever she was, I was not.
Whoever she was, I forgot
to ask, and she forgot to tell,
muffled in costumes she as well
rejected as a girl, resumed
– on my account? Are women doomed,
beasts that repeat ourselves, to rage
in youth against our own old age,
in age to circumscribe our youth
with self-despisal dressed as truth?
Am I 'Woman' to my water-
dwelling brown loquacious daughter,
corporeal exemplar of
her thirst for what she would not love?

1973

'I'm pregnant,' I wrote to her in delight
from London, thirty, married, in print. A fools-
cap sheet scrawled slantwise with one minuscule
sentence came back. 'I hope your child is white.'
I couldn't tear the pieces small enough.
I hoped she'd be black as the ace of spades,
though hybrid beige heredity had made
that as unlikely as the spun-gold stuff
sprouted after her neo-natal fur.
I grudgingly acknowledged her 'good hair,'
which wasn't, very, from my point of view.
'No tar-brush left,' her father's mother said.
'She's Jewish and she's white,' from her cranked bed
mine smugly snapped.
                              She's Black. She is a Jew.

Kate Hall

PSYCHIC HEALING

Being very upset
and
falling apart
I looked
in the psychic book
under
relationships breaking up.
Sprout seeds
it said
and eat them.
Well I didn't
have any seeds
not even
pumpkin seeds
and the health food shop
was shut.
But then
I remembered
that you can

sprout beans
so I did.
I nurtured
those beans
for days
watching them
swell
and burst open.
That
made me
even more miserable.

But I did
feel better
when I ate them.
I felt
it served
them right.

Caroline Halliday

SMELL OF MYSELF

the light, warm, golden-green   smell   (weeds, weeds in a ditch)
a smell of my daughter, my niece, myself
fingers (scratching, itching, rubbing?)   while a story is told,
or waiting for a bath to run, or early in bed
fingers smelling of   – my cunt, my own smell, fanny
                    wee, vagina. Bottom.

A small girl stands in the changing rooms, naked.
Two children stay the night and I bath them, skinny thighs,
a small folded inwards crease, a divide of flesh, neat, narrow, soft.

I am thinking of this little girl, myself, with a place she couldnt see
that had no name, just a bottom, all those years with no name for
                    – a clitoris, labia, vagina,
                    arsehole, skin, openings, flesh
                    Just a bottom –
delicately diverted from
                    (I remember separate itemised occasions,
remembered with caution and embarrassment . . .

that time in the summer house when
when I was four   and we were
my mother shadow round the doorway   so I knew we shouldnt
that time with my sisters in that bathroom
poured water through a funnel into
I didnt understand why it

                 . . . gradually accepted. Yes, I did touch
   myself.

a little bit of a smell, delicious,
with my daughter, my niece   and I begin to remember
begin to remember this smell

A struggle with myself to let physical sensation, sexual feelings into my
life, to knot together the body that feels duty, and passion, and 'why
doesnt it all come easily?'
and for that girl the unnameable part of herself, underneath, unseen,
wrapt up in secrecy and importance, non-existent, just a bottom –

Anger at this denial   gap   destruction   forced refusal of my own
threads, connections.

I looked with J, aged two, in the mirror at her cunt, telling her about it,
again. Her vagina is about an inch along. Looking at her I have a
   strong
sensation of having looked before. Small opening as wide and long as
the top bend of my little finger. Memory halts   yet I've seen it.
She peers over the edge of her body, pulling back the flesh to see
further, cant really see.

Unnamed   doesnt exist   whatever feelings this has   arent mine.

Unnamed   connect with   my body   breasts   something, vagina,
is humming like this typewriter   confused as all the words pushed
together   connect with feelings over and over again cut out dont
want to   the pressure   how he wants to fuck   no time for me and
yet I want my body wants   these places want   they are unnamed
dont exist surprise me dont connect –

Little children dont have the wrinkled, thin labia I have, they have
round, fat curves. R's as marked out and smiling as a mouth   lips,
a cheerful fanny.

I touched my arsehole yesterday   to sniff my fingers. Cant believe
Cant believe   how clear   clear a space that smell
   brings in
to my mind.

Light, robust comfortable smell. Firm.
I had this body of a swimmer, a girl, a secret to herself, and yet a
circle   knowing
            – the girl touches her arsehole to know what it smells like –
knowing how I loved that smell.   and again   and again.

You stroked my arsehole when we made love
I let myself be touched
the feeling magnifying itself in me
delicious, comforting.

I touched my arsehole yesterday and sniffed my fingers.
Cant believe how clear a space   that smell brings in.

THIS SPACE THE TIGER

Last night is clear in my mind
as I take my clothes off in my room
fresh rain falling its neat sound lightly
on leaves, streets, outside the open windows
my body is just itself tonight, patient
watches the room and remembers
filling the room with my skin, myself
my erotic self, naked
owned

Last night is fresh in my mind.
We'd walked into the closed park
stepped through the fence
we'd argued, I'd hit the desk so hard
my palm and fingers had stung
the tree I watched
moving a dark huge mass
We are always strangers
after each absence, strangers
who know each other
who know each other's bodies
I like my body with yours
You have a new lover but I don't care.
When we sat down on my yellow bed
I knew what your body could feel like
your skin tussling with mine

77

(your breasts over me
their sensitivity, and mine like fierceness)

you have a new lover
'Do you want to go to bed with me?'
I asked.

You slept in the next room because you were too
tired and I wanted to love myself –
self-erotic and all the energy for me
I said 'if you don't want me
this space won't be around
next time. Let me know'
I want a lover.
This woman is growing larger. Watch
yourself
Last night I loved myself, brown and silver,
in the music, I loved myself
wanting that space
pushed you over as if you were a fence
around my garden.

Each separate sensation of my
orgasm, clitoris, labia
each dark red muscle – supple
belonged to the dark room – mine
and the music was strong
don't misuse me, I said loudly, – watch
this space
vibrates, smooth skinned
If you said no, I thought,
there are other women I've never met
I am in love with myself and I have
touched myself this time and it is good
it is enough

Tonight there is a music of fine
raining/touching leaves, streets,
my body is quiet, dreaming on itself
you used to say   you have a beautiful body
my body remembers its beauty
you used to say   you are a wonderful lover
I am still here. I know all this is mine.

I saw the tiger yesterday, heavy, solid
knowing the weight of its body

intermittent, angry stripes
this texture of weight to hold
filling my mouth with colour
rolling against my body
I saw the weight of this body
myself
the danger of the paws
the face unreachable jowled.
My own glorious hide
grows bolder dangerously
towards this space
out of the garden.

Gillian Hanscombe

FRAGMENT

. . . so I bowed and nodded as best I could (though not as well as you)
and loved the people for loving you and admired the people for
admiring you and now and again I sensed you tease or tarry or find
something someone said just useful enough to keep and I was (if you'll
allow) so proud of you and pleased . . .

. . . and when we got back to whatever bed we were sharing then,
wherever it was, and were undressing ourselves (and each other – it is
the same) then one of us said to the other – well how did we do?
sideways, that is? were we all right? – yes my darling we were all
right, said the other; – but now let us see how we do face to face . . .

. . . and it was always odd (wasn't it?) how there was no afterwards
. . . the signs were there: the sweating, the racing of hearts, the heat . . .
and we were tired, inevitably . . . but it never actually stopped; there
was always a tongue somewhere on an eyebrow or cheek, a hand
somewhere, or arms that curved, legs that got muddled; always the
climbing or riding or scudding or falling; always the yes saying yes
and yes . . .

. . . and sometimes there was the wondering about who was who . . .

YOU LIKE ME

You like me wetbacked   you
like me curled in a

green wave tipping

                              you

like (any way) the

surf falling over   you
like the licking the
sand-smack sucking

                              and

spitting   you like the

sea's green muscle and
me in her rolling you
like the genius

                         of

art come true the

view the horizon that
lifts in the morning   you
like me there

                         at the

edge in the mouth of the

metaphor ready to be
feted with foam to be
gathered in armfuls

                              to be

broken open now

Debra Helme

YOUR CONTRADICTION

Don't tell me No with your mouth. Your whole
body is saying Yes. It forms into a memory of
mine. Five foot away, it dances with me,
writes my name with its twists. My hands are
unbuttoning your No. Your Nos pile up on
one side. Your smile is a five foot kiss
away, your fingers are looking for something
they lost. Don't say No. I can hear your blood
sing Yes, Yes, Yes. Your hand on my foot
burns through the sock. You leave scorch marks
all over.

Don't tell me No with your mouth while your
tongue knots with mine, while the skin of your
denial welds with mine. Your hands pull me
tighter, press the answer. You leap from your
small island of No, we swim in this Yes. You
leap five foot. Don't tell me No. I won't
repeat No: I'm an open Yes. No matter where
you put it, you cannot, and will not, hide your

                              Agree.

J.P. Hollerith

ALONE, WITH MUSIC

Alone, with music
With books
And words, words, words, words
All over my walls – where are *you*?
Traffic outside my house
I make sounds, filling my empty room.

So easy to be two that my old heritage
Feels hollow now.
I've lost
That wistful, tranquil, melancholy skill
Of being alone with myself
Complete. And if I never get things done
                              when I'm with you,
At least I'm happy.

Joy Howard

NOT A POET

Why can't we talk properly
about our lovers?
she asked me   meaning (of course)
improperly
why are we all so silent?
well I said   there's always

81

Poetry (and coughed a little nervously not
wanting to advertise)
do you ever . . .?
oh no she said quite
forcefully (not a poet   no)
I was thinking yesterday
she went on   of how
my lover's skin smells
like the sun
was on it   and on her hair
that smells too
of the sun . . .
but never a poet   she
oh no.

Maria Jastrzębska

WHICH OF US WEARS THE TROUSERS

Behind the liberal politeness
You're dying to know
Instead of the chat about societal attitudes
What you'd really like to ask is
Which of us in this relationship
Wears the trousers.

I'll tell you
Since you want to know so much
And since it's really very simple:
I do
And then again
She does
And then sometimes
Neither of us
Wears any trousers at all.

HALF POEM

this is a half poem
for the half of my heart
which beats fast when I'm frightened

and for the other half
which is braver
beating loudly
brimming over with anger
or love

for my life which is forever falling apart
in half pieces
before it comes together again as a whole
for the way there is usually more than one truth
and often more than two halves
for the halves that don't come in half sizes

this is a half poem
for the half of me that is most unacceptable
least public
at any given time
and for that half of the population
who've always had
the biggest half of my heart

TORBA/THE BAG

Made of worn, black leather
It's large and round
Old fashioned, not really elegant
A housewife's bag, a sensible bag
But there's a catch you wouldn't see
Unless you knew what you were looking for.

Her hands fumble with the bag
Feeling for the catch –
I know it's here I can remember it –
Find the spring which releases it
Opening a secret compartment.

In other homes
When the men got together over vodka
You'd hear about the war
Endless stories about the front
Which bored us children.
In our house
It was a matter of pride
Not to talk, never to boast

Except on someone else's behalf.
So we learned from my mother
About the day my father got shrapnel in his back
Carrying a wounded friend out of firing range,
But nothing about herself.

When she sits waiting for us
Crumpled and forlorn
When she answers 'I'll have to ask your father'
To everything I say
I don't know what to do
I want to shake her
Find the secret catch which can release
The woman
Who all through the Occupation
Crossed the streets of Warsaw
Carrying resistance papers
Hidden in her bag
And never got caught.

SEEING THE POPE ON TV

The figure of an old man
In flowing robes
Sunlight pouring on his head
Shining on his kindly face
His outstretched arms.

Not only that
But what it meant
When they elected a Pole – our Karolek
Chosen by the cardinals.
'Did you see the news
A Pole on TV?'

He could have been
An uncle or a grandfather
When he spoke in English,
I know the accent by heart
Recognised it straight away
The roll of the r's in 'corruption'.
He'd blessed the babies and the newly weds,
He was talking about the evil

Which threatens decent family life
I didn't smile
I knew it was me
He was talking about.

BILINGUAL

Under these words
Are the hidden words
I can't say to you –
Whichever way I face
There's always another language
One you don't know
One from which I sometimes translate
Words for you
Words you sometimes learn
Painfully
One at a time
But even then there's a gap
Even between words that are supposed to mean the same.

Under these words
Are the echoes of other words
Woven in brighter colours
Spoken more loudly
A different nourishment.
If I told you that other language runs
Swift as my own blood
Splashing and bubbling
Under the surface of our conversation
Runs like a river underground
Crying and thundering through silences

You can feel it
If you press your body to the ground
If I told you I want you
To press against these words
Would you feel its echoes?

Whichever way I face
Even between words which mean the same thing
There's a gap
An enormous space

It is a world of its own
Dazzling me
Wild rock torn apart
By sudden waterfalls
Rich source of my longings
World between worlds
I've paced up and down it
It is the loneliest place I know.

Jenn

YOU CAME

You came to use my washing machine
And did not leave until four days later.
There was no excuse.
I have a tumble dryer.

Jackie Kay

IF I DIG DEEP ENOUGH . . .

if I dig deep enough
I'll collect fragile sea shells
from my stomach
when I pick them out
they'll break
one childhood trust after another

if I skim my own surface
I'll gather surf to lather my own
matted hair foam crests to curl
newly forming dreads
I'll float for a living
without burrowing always

to the deep sea bottom
where no old treasures lie.

Melanie Kaye/Kantrowitz

KADDISH

and when I told the woman – a survivor, a fighter in the Warsaw
Ghetto Uprising – about the Holocaust conference in Maine, and how
many of the people there had known *nothing*, she said, *They still
know nothing.*

*

> *Yisgadal v'yiskadash sh'me rabbo,*
> *b'olmo deevro chiruseh v'yamlick*
> *malchuseh*

if I said kaddish for each one

if I were to mourn properly
I would not be done

If I were to mourn
each artist seamstress *schnorrer* midwife baker
each fiddler talker tailor shopkeeper
each *yente*   each Communist   each Zionist
each doctor pedlar beggar Bundist rabbi
each prostitute   each lesbian   each file clerk
each fighter   the old woman in the photograph from
Hungary   holding the hand of the child whose
socks droop   each Jew

> *b'chayechon uvyo-mechon, uv'chayey*
> *d'chol beys yisroel*

I would not be done   yet
it was more than death   was more   the people's
heart   a language I have
to study   to practice speaking with
old people   songs   to collect   transcribing
from records or from the few
who know   a culture   which might have died
in this country   which eats culture   a death
we call normal   a culture   *astonishing*
in its variety   a taste   a smell   a twist of song

87

that was   *Vilna*
           Odessa
           Cracow
           Covner-Gberna
           Warsaw
these were once Jewish sounds

*

                              baagolo uvizman koreev, v'imru
omen.

Tuesday my father died   Wednesday
the rabbi   who never met my father   met with us
my mother   my father's sisters   the daughters
5 minutes before the funeral was to begin
to prepare the eulogy   He asked
if my father had belonged to any organizations   if
people from   his place of business had come
and he said   since there were no sons
he   would say kaddish   for my father

and I did not tell the rabbi   my father was broken
before he died   I did not describe his twisted body   asbestos
in his lungs   I did not explain   my father worked
6 days plus 2 nights a week   paid
for my eyeglasses   cavities   penicillin shots
I did not say   he joined no temple

I did not say he loved the sound of Yiddish but
would not speak it
I did not mention he beat us   the children
but not his wife   I did not reveal his high point in life
a trip   with his buddies   to the Chicago World's Fair
in a '32 Ford   I did not say he changed his name   he was
Kantrowitz   he became Kaye   I did not say he built
a business   retail   and taught me
never cross a picket line

                              Y'he sh'meh rabbo m'vorach l'olam
                              ulolmey olmayo

I did not tell the rabbi   my father listened carefully
to all things Jewish

88

nor did I tell him
save your prayers

I said, *I will speak at this funeral*
and I did   to mourn him properly

*

v'yespo-ar v'yisromam v'yisnaseh
v'yishador v'yishal-lol

he taught me all men are equal before I knew
to suspect the words   before I learned
to fight with him to say   *people   all*
people   daddy   and please   don't say
girl

sh'med d'kud-sho b'reech-hu

About Israel   I always knew
Chanukah   we lit candles   said
no prayers   but got presents   red sweaters   ball bearings   sang
no songs   but *Hatikvah*   played on the menorah like
it was   our song   I knew I belonged to Jews
I knew   I was part of Israel

l'elo min col birchoso v'shiroso
tushb'choso v'nechemoso daamiron

and so I do
and so I am

and so   when I heard about children   women
families shot   stabbed at the table in   Shatilla
Sabra   I couldn't breathe
and I was   almost   too afraid   to mourn

let me be plain
Jews sent up flares
for christians   to kill by

let me absorb
yes   they are men   soldiers   also, my people   my father loved
all things Jewish   and should I disown?
I   who will be blamed   with the others   again

89

let me mourn   if anything
is holy   flesh
so readily torn   from the skeleton

let me rock   my body   like a scared child —
of what skin   what tongue   which people?
whose child is this?
the answer says if the child shall
live   die   suffer   kill

let me be strong as history
let me join those   who refuse
let there be time
let it be possible

>   *b'olmo y'imru omen. Y'he sh'lomo*
>   *rabbo min sh'mayo*

let no faction keep me
from those who suffer

let no faction keep me from those who needed a home
and found one

let no faction keep me from those
who need a home now

*

>   *v'chayim olenu v'al col yisroel.*
>   *v'imru omen.*

and in Rome   where Jesus the dead Jew is raised against us
as in Kansas   or California

a synagogue   blown up for being   a Jew place
a baby   blown up for being a   Jew baby
in *shul*   for the high holy days

>   *Oseh sholom bimrorev, hu'ya-aseh*

if there's a Jew alive   if a sin is always Jewish sin   this baby
paid   again   nothing is expiated   there is
blood in the camps   the bulldozers come to push
bodies   into hiding   this is what men do
Gemayel   is received at the UN   with applause
this is the Jewish problem

my father loved all things Jewish

a culture   *astonishing in its variety*   was

if I were to mourn properly
I would not be done

> *sholom olenu v'al col isroel. v'imru*
> *omen.*

kaddish, Jewish prayer for the dead, language: Aramaic. *schnorrer*, a moocher
yente, a gossip, someone who has to put her two cents in all the time
Bundist, member of the Jewish socialist organization *Hatikvah*, lit., 'hope'; the Israeli
national anthem *Gemayel*, President of Lebanon, head of the Christian Phalange Party
Note: All poems have sources, but with some, these sources are so immediate that it
seems only right to name them. *Kaddish* came to me first through the work of the
Argentinian Jew Mauricio Lansky, an artist whose series of prints depicts simply and
with extraordinary beauty face after face; each print has a number like a concentration
camp tattoo. Also crucial was Irena Klepfisz's long prose poem *Bashert* (published in
Sinister Wisdom 21 and in her book *Keeper of Accounts*). Jacobo Timerman's *The
Longest War: Israel In Lebanon* taught me to be more afraid of silence than of how
speech will be used against Jews. The many-faceted Israeli peace movement gives me
necessary inspiration and courage.

NAGASAKI DAY: LOS ALAMOS
for Michaele Uccella

where they built the bombs
(little boy for hiroshima
fat man for nagasaki)
was picked for its beauty
purple hills
aching sky

in a glass case in the museum at los alamos
is a tiny pile of sand from a card that says
sand from an island that
no longer exists

they explain.
before they made
fat man or little
boy. before they dropped them on
islands of little girls, big boys, women
of all sizes

they tested —
like men who rape their neighbors before

heading cross town –
spitting fire across their
own deserts, their own
people blind and cancerous
they blew up one of their
own islands   and said
it was good

in the courtyard of the museum at los alamos
are no statues of melting eyes, no
nagasaki cancer, no seared hiroshima
bodies of any size

just models
of little boy
and fat man
painted white
for good
to take pink hills from not-white
people of all sizes.   good
to blow up
islands of not-white people
of all sizes

here are no accidents
no mistakes.   they like
to stick their pins in maps
they like to pay for women
of certain sizes. or take
and not pay.
they like to decide. they
like to decide

and when people of all sizes, fat
girls, slight men, women
with broad shoulders pile
out of cattle cars
(some of course already dead)
to be stripped and searched and shaved
and tattooed blue numbers for a name
and murdered
or used
depending

here are men
of certain sizes

who like to click their heels
and point
you to the right
you to the left
you turn around let me
look at you

Meg Kelly

THE BOGEYWOMAN

though we may both pretend
(wear civilised masks)
behind the polite inquiries
and prefabricated smiles
lies a minefield of unexploded hostility

your daughter has never defused her eyes
they're a no-woman's land
guarded and barbed
with mistrust

those quick little eyes
saw the shut door;
the child's hand pushed
and found resistance
and the child's mind knew it had been excluded
shut out
while its mother kissed another

her eyes always tell me
(even now she's older)
you don't belong
you are the bogeywoman
come to steal my mummy

then love – all beautiful and fine –
becomes an ugly weapon
an axe, blunt-edged and greasy-handled,
hacking through the fragile framework
of her world

daddy's sad
mummy's mad

and the bogeywoman's here
drinking coffee
playing with the dog
smiling smiling smiling

Daisy Kempe

CHANGES

He no longer wears a plait.
He no longer keeps chickens.
The way the Radicals can.
No longer the same person
Or Man.

Now he wears short hair
Now he is the Department's Chairperson
Or Man.

His wife is no longer kept with the chickens.
She runs loose with no shoes.
The way Radical Wives can.
She does not look quite the same person.
Does not act quite according to plan.

He encourages her freedom.
Admires her aplomb.
(He calls her Mom)
He buys her new shoes.
He discovers
She has outgrown them.

He discovers
She has discovered another life.
He discovers
She has discovered
Another
Radical Wife.

He wishes they still kept chickens.

Tina Kendall

VIRGINS AND PEACHES

so there were peaches firm
to the touch but furry
and the room was all white
full of women chatting together
and touching together but

she did not see the women only
peaches only fruit

one woman flicked a button
lit the stereo started   music
started swaying she was
swaying to the music watching
peaches seeing visions lost
all contact

and the music was loud
and urgent in its claim
that women's love you've
got to know to know but
all she knew was she was
young and black the centre
of this soft and fragrant
peach yet standing back out
from all those who are milling
mixing mingling she sighs

but secretly she's glad
she's a peach, her skin
is soft and it is glowing
all is glowing don't want
love don't want to be   in
love yet just want to be
in touch a virgin is
a virgin (take your time
girl) is a virgin
to the touch

OVERDRAWN

she sent me monthly love-
statements — an assessment
of the way things stood —
i queried what i saw
what was this standing order
why was my credit so low
resulting then in dreadful
debit readings making me out to be
a bad risk a lousy investment
since i am permanently overdrawn

Kim

LESBIAN STRENGTH

When I woke up this morning
My lover was gone
I wasn't surprised
Cos I knew things were wrong
We just kept on fighting
We couldn't agree
I blamed things on her
She blamed them on me
We fought in the bedroom
We fought in the street
She liked to eat beans
I liked to eat meat
I wanted a doggie
For runs in the park
She said it would smell
And would have a loud bark
She wanted a cat
I said they were boring
But when I turned round
She'd put a cat door in
Still she's taken the cat
And the car and the telly
While I sit alone
With all knots in my belly
I know I'm a lesbian

And meant to be strong
But
Right now
I feel bloody awful

Linda King

SPOTTING LESBIAN SOCKS

I
should have known
She
Was a Lesbian
before
She told
Us
said Shirl to Gladys
only
those kind of women
wear
socks
underneath
dress hems
Yeah I knew
she looked
butch
said Gladys to Shirl
wearing
socks
without
boots
It
would've been different
if
her socks
were frilly and lacy
then
I
wouldn't have had
to face
her

sexuality
Oh God
It's crazy said Shirl to Gladys
I mean
she looked just
like one of
us
But then
Oh God
Why am I
so confused
Oh don't be
so boring
said Shirl to Gladys
You can tell Carl
all
about it
tonight
He'll be amused
I mean
it
might be a turn on
then
you'll get a screw
Don't be so cheeky
Gladys said Shirl
This is serious
I've got to
be able to tell
us
from them
Otherwise
I won't know
who
to draw the line
with
when I'm fooling around
You mean
like when you
put
your arm around me chuck
said Gladys
and

touch my knees
when
we are sitting
on the bus
Hey, don't worry
about it
said Shirl to Gladys
that's just
us
being
girls
I mean
Carl and Earl
hug
each other
after
football
and
you know
how Earl likes
to dress up
so we can play
girls
No, I mean, he's my pal
said Shirl to Gladys
It's the girls
I'm worried about
I almost took her
to be
one of us

Irena Klepfisz 🖋

ETLEKHE VERTER OYF MAME-LOSHN/
A FEW WORDS IN THE MOTHER TONGUE

עטלעכע ווערטער אויף מאמע-לשון

lemoshl: for example

di kurve   the whore
a woman who acknowledges her passions

99

di yidene   the Jewess   the Jewish woman
ignorant   overbearing
let's face it: every woman is one

di yente   the gossip   the busybody
who knows what's what
and is never caught off guard

di lezbianke   the one with
a roommate   though we never used
the word

dos vaybl   the wife
or the little woman
　　　　*

in der heym   at home
where she does everything to keep
yidishkayt alive

yidishkayt   a way of being
Jewish   always arguable

in mark   where she buys
di kartofl un khalah
(yes, potatoes and challah)

di kartofl   the material counter-
part of *yidishkayt*

mit tsibeles   with onions
that bring *trern tsu di oygn*
tears to her eyes   when she sees
how little it all is
veyniker un veyniker
less and less

di khalah   braided
vi ihr hor far der khasene
like her hair before the wedding
when she was *aza sheyn meydl*
such a pretty girl

di lange shvartse hor
the long black hair
di lange shvartse hor
　　　　*

a froy kholmt   a woman
dreams *ihr ort oyf der velt*

her place in this world
un zi hot moyre   and she is afraid
so afraid of the words
kurve
yidene
yente
lezbianke
vaybl

zi kholmt   she dreams   די קורווע
un zi hot moyre   and she is afraid   די יידענע
ihr ort   די יענטע
di velt   די לעזביאַנקע
di heym
der mark   דאָם ווײַבל

a meydl kholmt   אַ מיידל
a kurve kholmt
a yidene kholmt   אַפֿרוי
a yente kholmt
a lezbianke kholmt

a vaybl kholmt
di kartofl
di khalah

yidishkayt

zi kholmt
di hor
di lange shvartse hor   זי חלומט

zi kholmt   זי חלומט
zi kholmt
zi kholmt   זי חלימט

FROM THE MONKEY HOUSE AND OTHER CAGES

THE VOICE OF THE FIRST MONKEY

The voices are those of female monkeys born and raised in a zoo

Monkey I

1
from the beginning
she was always dry   though
she'd press me close
prying open my lips:

the water warm
the fruit   sour   brown
apples bruised and soft.

hungry for dark   i'd sit
and wait   devour dreams
of plain sun and sky
large leaves   trunks   dark
and wet with sweet thick sap.

                    but morning
brought back the space
and cement   her weakened
body   my head against her
breast: my mouth empty.

2
yet she was   all
my comfort: her sharp
ribs against my cheek
her bony fingers   rough
in fluffing me dry.

she showed me   all
the space   the changing
colors outside   then

pulled me back   forced
me to sit with her
in a shadowy corner.

on certain clear days
she'd shrug   hold me in the sun:
her fur lacked smoothness
her body warmth.

3

in the midst of heat
they took me   with smooth
round strokes   and hushing
sounds.

she sat silent
at first   sniffing their sweat
their stale breath   then leaped on one
her eyes wide   her claws poised and sharp.
he grunted   deep
from within   an empty cavern
echoing the storm outside
flicked her off   and dragged me out.

i could hear her sound
as if a sea lion roared
then becoming tired

drowned.

4

their space was smaller
cramped and low   the air
foul   with their sweat
their salt.

and their motions
were sharp   as they spread me out
clamped me down
for the opening probe.

i did not move
just sucked my breath
with each new venture   into my deepest parts
and then   with time
i became   a dark dull color
a gray rain   blending
with the liquid   of her eyes.

5

when they returned me
the air was ice:
bare branches   meshed
against a hard   dark sky.

i sat alone.   we were
separate now   though

she was still there
in the cage   next to mine.
her fur was stiff   her nostrils spread
she eyed me   circled
her back arched   ready for attack.

later   as the food was dropped
she leaped forward
hissed   snatched bits of fruit
from my side   of the bars.

6
a day   and a day
the pools   dead and dry
i'd sit and stare
into the cold   into the empty trees.

but she seemed   at rest
pressing against the bars
eyes closed   alone   on the other side.
only when i ate   she'd look sharp at me
her mouth moving
as i swallowed   each bite

and as night blackened us
she'd gather her scraps
enclose herself   in her arms.

7
the male   sleek-furred
was young   and active
when they forced him through to me.

i stayed in place   all
eyes and ready   while she leaped
in frenzy   retreated to the furthest wall.
he kept his distance
ignoring her   ignoring me
ate small morsels   tumbled
stared outside.

the ice was thawing
the pools filled and quiet.
i listened   as the soil
sopped   became mud
deep   and brown.

8

soon the trees budded   and i
pinked   softened   and presented.
he penetrated   withdrew
penetrated   withdrew
over   and over
till i was dry
and hard.
          she sat
relaxed and quiet
began to chew apples
slowly picking out
each black seed.

9

               later
i cramped   shrivelled
then opened   wide   wide
my flesh thin and stretched
till: it burst forth
a thing   so strange
so pale   and hairless
a mass of flesh   separate from mine.

and through the heat
and heavy trees   the sound of water
the light of the moving sun:
the male ate regularly
the small one sucked
i mashed the sour fruit
between my lips.

she watched us all
as we would swallow
hoard   any piece of rind
or seed   that she could find.

10

the male was taken:
i turned my back.
the small one was taken:
i was held to one side.

and again   and again
the trees emptied again

the soil became hard
then became soft again.

and the cage is   all
mine   and i have myself:
touching my fur
pulling my face

while she moves so slowly
without any sound
eating   pacing
twisting her arms   around the hard bars.

11
sometimes at night   i watch
her asleep: the rigid bones
the thinned out fur

and i can see clearly
the sky   the bars
as we sat together
in a spot of sun
and she   eyes closed
moved me
moved me
to the sounds of the waters
lapping
in the small   stone pools
outside.

THEY DID NOT BUILD WINGS FOR THEM

they did not build wings for them
the unmarried aunts;   instead they
crammed them into old maids' rooms
or placed them as nannies with
the younger children;   mostly they
ate in the kitchen, but sometimes
were permitted to dine with the family
for which they were grateful and
smiled graciously as the food was passed.
they would eat slowly never filling
their plates and their hearts would

sink at the evening's end when it was
time to retreat into an upstairs corner.

but there were some who did not smile
who never wished to be grafted on
the bursting houses.   these few remained
indifferent to the family gatherings
preferring the aloneness of their small rooms
which they decorated with odd objects
found on long walks.   they collected
bird feathers and skulls unafraid to clean
them to whiteness;   stones which resembled
humped bears or the more common tiger and
wolf: dried leaves whose brilliant colors
never faded;   pieces of wood still covered
with fresh moss and earth which retained
their moisture and continued flourishing.
these they placed by their dresser mirror
in arrangements reminiscent of secret rites
or hung over delicate watercolors of unruly
trees whose branches were about to snap
with the wind.

it happened sometimes that among these
one would venture even further.   periodically
would be heard vague tales of a woman
withdrawn and inaccessible suddenly disappearing
one autumn night leaving her room bare
of herself.   women gossiped about a man.
but eventually word would come back
she had moved north to the ocean and lived
alone.   she was still collecting
but now her house was filled with crab
and lobster shells;   discolored claws
which looked like grinning south american
parrots trapped in fish nets decorated
the walls;   skulls of unidentifiable
creatures were arranged in geometric patterns
and soft reeds in tall green bottles
lined the window sills.   one room
in the back with totally bare walls
was a workshop.   here she sorted colored
shells and pasted them on wooden boards

in the shape of common flowers.   these she sold
without sentiment.

such a one might also disappear inland.
rumor would claim she had travelled in
men's clothing.   two years later it would
be reported she had settled in the woods
on some cleared land.   she ran a small farm
mainly for supplying herself with food
and wore strangely patched dresses and shawls
of oddly matched materials.   but aloneness
was her real distinction.   the house was neat
and the pantry full.   seascapes and pastoral
scenes hung on the walls.   the garden was
well kept and the flower beds clearly defined
by color: red   yellow   blue.   in the woods
five miles from the house she had an orchard.
here she secretly grafted and crossed varieties
creating singular fruit of shades and scents
never thought possible.   her experiments rarely
failed   and each spring she waited eagerly to see
what new forms would hang from the trees.
here the world was a passionate place and she
would visit it at night baring her breasts
to the moon.

FRADEL SCHTOK

Yiddish writer. B. 1890 in Skale, Galicia. Emigrated to New York in 1907.
Became known when she introduced the sonnet form into Yiddish poetry.
Author of *Erzeylungen* [Stories] (1919), a collection in Yiddish. Switched to
English and published *For Musicians Only* (1927). Institutionalized and died
in a sanitarium around 1930.

'Language is the only homeland'
Czeslaw Milosz

They make it sound easy: some disjointed
sentences   a few allusions   to
mankind. But for me   it was not
so simple   more like   trying
to cover the distance   from here
to the corner   or between two sounds.

Think of it: *heym*   and   *home*   the meaning

108

the same   of course   exactly
but the shift   in vowel   was the ocean
in which I drowned.

I tried. I did   try.
First held with Yiddish   but you
know   it's hard. You write   *gas*
and   *street*   echoes back.
No resonance. And – let's face it –
memory falters.
You try to keep track of the difference
like *got* and *god*   or *hoyz* and *house*
but they blur   and you start using
alley   when you mean *gesele*   or *avenue*
when it's a *bulevar.*

And before you know it
you're on   some alien path
standing   before a brick house
the doorframe   slightly familiar.
Still   you can't place it
exactly. Passers-by   stop.
Concerned   they speak   but you've
heard   all this before   the vowels
shifting   up and down   the subtle
change   in the guttural sounds
and now   it's nothing more
nothing   more   than   babble.
And so   you accept it.
You're lost. This time   you really
don't know   where you are.

Land or sea   the house floats before you.
Perhaps you once sat   at that window
and it was home   and looked out
on that *street or gesele.* Perhaps
it was a dead end   perhaps a short cut.
Perhaps not.
A movement by the door. They stand there
beckoning   mouths open and close:
Come in! Come in! I understood   it was
a welcome. *A dank! A dank!*
I said   till I heard the lock
snap   behind me.

Jennifer Krebs

SHORT BLACK HAIR

My short black hair. My sister studying to be a hairdresser cuts it shorter still. Much to my parents' horror. My mother mumbles: you look like a man. You look like your great aunt Adele, my father tells me.

Wasn't she the poet? Aunt Adele.

No. She was a bookkeeper. Although she might have written a poem or two. Bad poems. Pure emotion. Rhymes without meter, rhythm.

Aunt Adele. Foremother I never met. Aunt Adele. I probably don't look a thing like her.

On my father's side of the family there were two unmarried women.

Grandma's sister Paula, the tailor. I met her twice. She sewed me a brown corduroy dog with floppy ears and a black button nose. I named her Cleo. I still have Cleo somewhere in my bedroom in my parents' house.

Grandpa's sister Adele. The poet.

My grandma kneads bread dough. Tells me about the world. Before. In Germany. Waltzes and polkas and farms and trips to Frankfurt. My father as a baby. Grandma's eleven sisters and brothers. Mainly sisters. Grandpa getting drafted in World War I. Grandma lost two brothers in that war. She met and married Grandpa after he came back.

All my grandpa's brothers and sisters married after the war. Except Adele.

Why?

A cousin tells me Adele fell in love with a Gentile poet or teacher. They wrote poems to each other. Her father Levi forbade her to intermarry.

My grandma doesn't understand the question. She just didn't marry.

My grandpa died before I had time to ask.

My father says my cousin is wrong. There was no poet. Where did she/ I get such ideas? My father thinks the inquiry is pointless.

But I'm not getting married. I'm getting my hair cut. Short. These questions are vital. My aunt's life is vital. Her life is denied.

Germany killed her.

Except a poem. She wrote in Theresienstadt. A poem, I am told, about the winds. A poem. A prayer for the messiah.

My father wants to know why I want to be a writer. To contribute to magazines? Time, Commentary, National Geographic? Write about politics – after all I studied International Affairs.

No.

They shaved Adele's hair off to do brain surgery. Incised a cross in her skull to find out why she stopped walking. A cross in her skull right above her spine.

They opened her up. Saw her grey brain matter. Same as anyone's grey brain matter. Sewed her back up. Still didn't know why she couldn't walk any more.

She couldn't walk. She couldn't go.

My cousin says I should be fair to the doctors at Marburg. It was a university hospital. Not a Nazi hospital. They were scholars, surgeons. Not Nazi quacks. But it was Nazi Germany. They cut a cross in her head. She wore a cross of scar tissue for the rest of her life.

She couldn't walk.

She stopped walking because they took her job away. They took her job away because she was a Jewish woman. And because it was 1933.

She couldn't go.

She went to the town school through the eighth grade. Then she went to a business high school. A bookkeeper. An accountant. She became the merchandise manager of the local chain of grocery stores. She was efficient. She was competition for any man.

They fired her. On the way home from work she collapsed in the street. She never walked again.

Or maybe she did. My father can't remember. Maybe she did walk a little bit now and again. Maybe.

The family got her a wheelchair.

I took care of a woman in a wheelchair for three years. Twice a week. I was a college student. I needed money. She asked me: can you push a wheelchair? I said I'd try. She had multiple sclerosis.

I spent two Christmases with her. Her family was far away. She spent

111

Christmases with Jews. I got her up in the morning. Dressed her in her newest wraparound skirt. Took her to the toilet. Opened her Christmas presents. Spoonfed her turkey and cranberry sauce and pearl onions.

Tried to help. Aunt Adele. Help. Felt sick. Adele. Screamed. When I left.

In 1941, my grandpa secured visas for himself, his father, his wife, his children to the U.S. In 1941, they didn't let Adele out. Or they didn't want Adele in.

She couldn't walk. She couldn't go.

My grandpa, grandma, father, aunts, great-grandfather left. Adele.

Stayed behind in Germany. Short black hair. Wheelchair.

My father says she screamed. Short black hair. Alone. Screamed. Alone. When they left. They left.

They moved the rest of the Jews in town into her house. Her father Levi's house. My family's house. A woman came every day to take care of Adele.

A Gentile woman. Came every day for a year. She got Adele up in the morning. Cooked. Fed. Got Adele ready to celebrate Jewish Holidays. They didn't celebrate Jewish Holidays in 1941.

I fed her turkey and cranberry sauce and pearl onions.

My grandpa worked as a painter in New York City nine years before he and his brothers made enough money to buy a farm in upstate New York like the farm they had in Germany.

My grandma bakes bread. Feeds the cats. Sleeps under German quilts. Eats on linen tablecloths her mother embroidered.

My father is a mechanical engineer turned farmer. Returned to farmer. Like his father. I write.

Aunt Adele wrote poetry.

They put her on a train to Theresienstadt with her wheelchair and the rest of the Jews. She wrote a letter to the woman who took care of her after my family left.

I got a letter last week from the woman with multiple sclerosis. She's got a new college student working for her. Who writes. Who wrote the letter for her. She's well. Except the bed sores. Except she can't move by herself.

I sent her a letter yesterday. I'm writing. I'll send her a story or a poem. Soon. Next letter.

Adele sent a poem to the woman who took care of her. She was a writer. Even in the concentration camp. She wrote. She wrote about the winds. She prayed for the messiah.

They tossed her body in an unmarked grave.

She had short black hair.

I'm getting my hair cut. Short.

Jacqueline Lapidus

KIDNAPPING II

Pale lunar landscape of the dunes, my hand
caressing you, I could drive all the way
to Boston if I didn't have a mand-
atory date in half an hour. Play
time, stolen. I'm doing sixty, how
can I keep my mouth on the road if you
look at me like that? 'Turn here. Now
go uphill to the top and park.' The view
stretches, shimmering like a mirage,
clear over Pilgrim Lake to Provincetown.
Whatever we may lack, it isn't courage.
Greedily we kiss, again and again
and again. Oh, you're a handsome
woman, worth a few risks and a queen's ransom!

Joan Larkin

TRANSLATION

No truthful way to say just
how the wood thrush swayed on the limb
repeating her short phrase,
your hair threaded my fingers,
your back against my palm, your neck —
salt fallen into honey.
The hieroglyphic
of a crisp hair in my hand.

A THREAD

Your sister died —

Did you let in your own grief
or did you wind yourself up tight
on the spool of your mother's pain

Are you still taking care of your mother

Tell me the story
again
so we both can hear
how it all comes out

RAPE

After twenty years I want to call it that, but was it?
I mean
it wasn't all his fault, I mean
wasn't I out there on 8th Street,
wandering around looking for someone to fill the gap where my center
    would have been?
Didn't I circle the same block over & over until he saw me?
Wasn't I crying when he came along & said *Don't do that, cops see me
    with a white girl crying* —
I'm sorry. Didn't I say *I'm sorry,* & didn't I smile?
Didn't I walk with him, dumb, to the Hotel Earle,
didn't I drink with him in his room,
didn't I undress myself in the stare of a yellow bulb?
Didn't I drink — what was it I drank?
Didn't I drink enough to be numb for a long time?
Didn't I drink myself into a blackout?

Was it rape, if when I lay there letting him fuck me I started to feel
sore & exhausted & said *Stop,*
first softly, then screaming
Stop, over & over?
And if he was too drunk to hear me,
or if he heard me but thought, *Girls never mean it when they say stop,*
was that rape? Was it rape if he meant well
or was too drunk to hear me, was it rape
if he kept repeating *Girl, you can fuck*
& not really meaning any harm?

114

I think I remember that the room was green & black,

the small bulb dangling from a cord,
the bed filthy.
I don't exactly remember.
I know I had no pleasure, but lay there; I don't think he forced me.
It was just that he wouldn't stop when I asked him to.
He didn't take my money.
It may have been his booze I drank.
It may have been sort of a date.
He wrote his number on half a matchbook & said
Call Joe if you need him – I guess he was Joe.

Did I walk home?
Did I have any money?
Was it me who bought the booze?
Maybe I took a cab.
Was it 2:00 a.m., or safe daylight
when I climbed the five flights,
spent, feeling the tear tracks & pounded cervix,
the booze still coating me, my nerves not yet awake, stripped &
    screaming.
I climbed to my place, five flights,
somehow satisfied,
somehow made real by the pain.

Was it rape, then?

ORIGINS

It was a party; I had on my party dress.
There was something wrong in Grandpa's friend's throat.
I kept him waiting outside the bathroom
while I read *Mother West Wind 'When' Stories*.
When Mama yelled at me to *Make it fast*,
I wiped. I flushed. I came out on the landing
holding the blue book behind my back.
His lighted cigar was the red eye of an animal.
He reached a hand up – big, spotted like an animal –
under the short skirt of my party dress.
I felt pleasure, and I felt afraid of the hand.
Nice girl, he was smiling,
and the red eye shook and smelled like a cigar.

115

This was at the top of some stairs —
what house was it?
Were there stairs on Westminster Avenue?
How little was I? I remember. Little.
I said, *Mama, the man touched me.*
No, she said. She was worried
about the party; she was serving
a tray of green things and pink things.
She explained the facts to me quickly.
No, she said.
The man is a nice old man.

GENEALOGY

I come from alcohol.
I was set down in it like a spark in gas.
I lay down dumb with it, I let it erase what it liked.
I played house with it, let it dress me, undress me.
I exulted, I excused.
I married it. And where it went, I went.
I gave birth to it.
I nursed, I plotted murder with it.
I laid its table, paid its promises.
I lived with it wherever it liked to live:
in the kitchen, under the bed, at the coin laundry,
out by the swings, in the back seat of the car,
at the trashed Thanksgiving table.
I sat with it in the blear of tv.
I sat where it glittered, carmine,
where it burned in a blunt glass,
where it stood in a glittering lineup on the bar.
I saw it in the dull mirror, making up my face,
in the week-end silence,
in the smashed dish, in the slammed car door,
in the dead husband, the love.
Alcohol in the torn journal.
Alcohol in the void mirror.
My generations are of alcohol
and all that I could ever hope to bear.

Rebecca Lewin

IN THIS DIVORCE

A new wife for the woman
who was my wife
and no words between us now.

A new woman
in my woman's bed,
and she in the other's.

What of the futures torn
by the changes,
what of the minds that must now turn
away from what was once projected certainty?

There are no children
in this divorce,
no lawyers, no in-laws, and yet
the lines are drawn deep between us,
all the webs reaching into each other's lives,
all the hooks and toys left behind,
the memories that injure,
and still the love, still crystalline between us,
for how could that break?

How could it have broken?

THE LESBIAN DIVORCE

If I could conjure you precisely
would that relieve me of the loss?
Repeatedly I say to myself,
But I thought this was going to happen,
we were going to do that.

I must now believe in the death
of my old delighted hopes and certainties
and forget the promises
and remember we both tried
and forgive your confusion
and not hate her who took what was most precious
from me.

Oh, lesbian divorce! You death,
you fooler! It was women I believed in
as if we would hurt each other less
than men hurt us.

Sky of my room,
air between the walls,
with what will I fill you now
that I can love no one,
can kiss no one honestly?
I am wide as the unknown distances above
and my space is as black and frightening.
I could yell or paint or turn the music up
or dance or lie down on the rug
or invite the ones who want me home.

But my lover was a child
and I am a child
and my years are collecting behind me
like the mysteries I love and fear
that are beyond the sunset,
and I'm not ready to rise up born again
like a child learning to walk,
and I'm not ready to have lost her,
and I can't say to the world, *Help me, I am divorced,*
I am divorced!

They would not even believe
we had ever been married.

Audre Lorde

NOW THAT I AM FOREVER WITH CHILD

How the days went
while you were blooming within me
I remember each upon each —
the swelling changed planes of my body
and how you first fluttered, then jumped
and I thought it was my heart.

How the days wound down
and the turning of winter

I recall with you growing heavy
against the wind. I thought
now her hands
are formed, and her hair
has started to curl
now her teeth are done
now she sneezes.
Then the seed opened
I bore you one morning just before spring
My head rang like a fiery piston
my legs were towers between which
A new world was passing.

Since then
I can only distinguish
one thread within running hours
You, flowing through selves
toward You.

STATIONS

Some women love
to wait
for life   for a ring
in the June light   for a touch
of the sun to heal them   for another
woman's voice   to make them whole
to untie their hands
put words in their mouths
form to their passages   sound
to their screams   for some other sleeper
to remember   their future   their past.

Some women wait for their right
train   in the wrong station
in the alleys of morning
for the noon to holler
the night come down.

Some women wait for love
to rise up
the child of their promise
to gather from earth

what they do not plant
to claim pain for labor
to become
the tip of an arrow   to aim
at the heart of now
but it never stays.

Some women wait for visions
that do not return
where they were not welcome
naked
for invitations to places
they always wanted
to visit
to be repeated.

Some women wait for themselves
around the next corner
and call the empty spot peace
but the opposite of living
is only not living
and the stars do not care.

Some women wait for something
to change   and nothing
does change
so they change
themselves.

NAMING THE STORIES

Otter and quaking aspen
the set of a full cleansing moon
castle walls crumble
in silence
visions trapped by the wild stone
lace up the sky   pale electric fire
no sound
but a soft expectation of birds
calling the night home.

Half asleep   bells
mark a butterfly's birth
over the rubble

I crawl into dawn
corn woman bird girl sister
calls from the edge of a desert
where it is still night
to tell me her story
survival.

Rock speaks   a rooster language
and the light is broken
clear.

EVERY TRAVELER HAS ONE VERMONT POEM

Spikes of lavender aster under Route 91
hide a longing or confession
'I remember when air was invisible'
from Chamberlin Hill down to Lord's Creek
tree mosses point the way home.

Two nights of frost
and already the hills are turning
curved green against the astonished morning
sneeze-weed and ox-eye daisies
not caring   I am a stranger
making a living choice.

Tanned boys I do not know
on their first proud harvest
wave from their father's tractor
one smiles as we drive past
the other hollers
nigger
into cropped and fragrant air.

ETHIOPIA
for Tifa

Seven years without milk
means everyone dances for joy
on your birthday
but when you clap   your hands
break at the wrist

and even grandmother's ghee
cannot mend
the delicate embroideries
of bone.

CALL

Holy ghost woman
stolen out of your name
Rainbow Serpent
whose faces have been forgotten
Mother   loosen my tongue or adorn me
with a lighter burden
Aido Hwedo is coming.

On worn kitchen stools and tables
we are piecing our weapons together
scraps of different histories
do not let us shatter
any altar
she who scrubs the capitol toilets, listening
is your sister's youngest daughter
gnarled Harriet's anointed
you have not been without honor
even the young guerrilla has chosen
yells as she fires into the thicket
Aido Hwedo is coming.

I have written your names on my cheekbone
dreamed your eyes   flesh my epiphany
most ancient goddesses   hear me
enter
I have not forgotten your worship
nor my sisters
nor the sons of my daughters
my children watch for your print
in their labors
and they say Aido Hwedo is coming.

I am a Black woman   turning
mouthing your name as a password
through seductions   self-slaughter

and I believe in the holy ghost
mother
in your flames beyond our vision
blown light through the fingers of women
enduring   warring
sometimes outside your name
we do not choose all our rituals
Thandi Modise   winged girl of Soweto
brought fire back home in the snout of a mortar
and passes the word from her prison cell   whispering
Aido Hwedo is coming.

Rainbow Serpent who must not go
unspoken
I have offered up the safety of separations
sung the spirals of power
and what fills the spaces
before power unfolds or flounders
in desirable nonessentials
I am a Black woman   stripped down
and praying
my whole life has been an altar
worth its ending
and I say Aido Hwedo is coming.

I may be a weed in the garden
of women I have loved
who are still
trapped in their season
but even they shriek
as they rip burning gold from their skins
Aido Hwedo is coming.

We are learning by heart
what has never been taught
you are my given   fire-tongued
Oya   Seboulisa   Mawu   Afrekete
and now we are mourning our sisters
lost to the false hush of sorrow
to hardness and hatchets and childbirth
and we are shouting
Rosa Parks and Fannie Lou Hamer
Assata Shakur and Yaa Asantewa

my mother and Winnie Mandela are singing
in my throat
the holy ghosts' linguist
one iron silence broken
Aido Hwedo is calling
calling
your daughters are named
and conceiving
Mother   loosen my tongue
or adorn me
with a lighter burden
Aido Hwedo is coming.

Aido Hwedo is coming.

Aido Hwedo is coming.

Aido Hwedo: The Rainbow Serpent; also a representation of all ancient divinities who
must be worshipped but whose names and faces have been lost in time.

Maia

KITCHEN TO RAINFOREST

Prowling the kitchen again
among grit and week-old dishes,
I come across the stewpot sprouting
long-haired molds, flaming silver
manes around each ricegrain, the holy
dregs dressed up to kill.

It strikes me this wilderness
need not be conquered.

I imagine every pan and bowl thus furred.
Birdnests in the curtains. Mouseturds merrily
scattered across the porcelain, undisturbed.
I imagine letting go of this
compulsion to war
with life-forms not my next of kin.

What harm if the elements
come and go as it pleases them?
Why interfere, for instance,

with dust's mild ambition
simply to come to rest?

This house fifty years from now
will have its way with me anyhow. In the bedroom
sheets will wear themselves out
beneath my sleep, the windowglass
rubbed thin with looking
will hold my face a few years more.
And then I will disappear.

It is beginning already, see
the air is eating my fingers and toes
like a lover I want to give in to, not
a simple death but

radical metamorphosis: kitchen
to rainforest, scoured pot to exotic
fur and feathers.

THE LONG REACH

I stand here
forty years down the row
of plucked beans,
fattening my repertoire with
snatched-up melodies, wisecracks,
homilies of the crow,
sweet to my ear but
sharp as grass on the tongue, year by year
stored up like calcium
in the whorling bone.

Leaves flame again, my heart
like a sunflower following.
Frisking the stalks, I glean the hard
fruit left that year
when the harvester slashed and slashed
its claw too crude to gather.

In the dirt I dig up
a jigsaw of broken mirror, my face
revealing cracks, moonmarks

on the perfect disk, fore-
shadows of a comet
returning in the year of my death.

What do I care?

The long reach   winter
for spring, night/for
morning. Old grief
waters the newborn eyelids.

I come from that country
where hungry is a word learned early.
Hungry, I said,
five-year-old hands outstretched to the cupboard,
mother's sharp arms
closing around a private emptiness . . .
Hungry, hungry, hungry, I said,
she could never fill me up.
And later the men came
sniffing around her tragic skin with their
magician's knack for disappearance
leaving me empty-handed every time . . .

Childhood's gone
through the kiln, the crazed
clay bowl holds water now.
I have given up prohibitions, see
I go barefoot and bold
among the holiest moments, each season
shaking more and more into me,
the smallest pocket bursting with seed, the whole
orchard twigging through my head, I keep
what I need.

If crows fall
out of the nest too soon
let me catch them.

Mothercrow laughs harshly
from her easy perch in the corn.
It's a good joke.
Neither blessed with leaves nor wings, I am
burdened with language, she
takes pity now and again, gives me back

the agony of words
as a sequence of pure right notes.

I reach down the row
fingering beanshoots, whistling
and dancing for my dinner, ragged feathers
shooing terror
to the edge, to the edge like
that wrecked machine on the field's margin
rusting and raging into the dirt.

When I am penniless,
my coat poorly woven and worn, midnight
cutting its cold
knife clear through me,
I lie face down and pray to the roots . . .

I don't know why
angels lean down the light
to clothe me, the very
ground I stand on carries me
back to the sky.

Caeia March

A MESSAGE TO THE COLLECTIVE

I would like to go
to a meeting where my voice
is heard
and talk about my
struggles to become a lesbian writer

I had two babies over ten years ago.

I would like to know you to let you near enough to listen
to my talking, my joys, or speaking bitterness.

I had two babies over ten years

Those of you who say I had a choice
You with no child care. Talking fast
at me with your explanations.
Mothers are well trained to listen

I had two babies over

you want me to hear you
don't you? You have stories to tell
of your lives. I have time.

I had two babies

You talk about your struggles
how to gather your thoughts together
your ideas, the colours in your minds
You move as quickly as you dare through
the boring items on the agenda. Not terribly
interested you say in

I had two

organising childcare. Much more
fascinated if I move on to discuss
the techniques of short story writing

I had

and the content and form of
political fiction, poetry

I.

I have to go now because
my children are waiting.

Judith McDaniel 🖋

LA ESPERANZA

My children
he told me and I could see
the little one
belly sagging out
from a clean torn t-shirt
are the decoration
belly swollen
but not quite distended
child eyes look at me
knowing too much
to be quite starved

of my home he waved
his hand across the dusty
yard the barren doorsill
the smell of nothing
from the woodfire in the corner.
My children are the decoration of my home.

Christian McEwen ✍

INHERITANCE

Good and better, good and better. Best. My father was the best.
He had a brain. He went to Cambridge and he got a First. What does
your father do? How big's your house?

My house is big. It has a hundred rooms. My father's best. He used to
know the Queen. My family's better. It is not like yours. My life is
different. I am not to blame.

My father was a baronet. He had a brain. He got depressed and so he
used to drink. My mother prayed. There wasn't any cash. The doctors
came and then they went away.

Good and better, good and better. Best. My mother's good and I'm a
clever girl. I am so tidy in my clean white tights. My father's getting
better very fast.

We have our rituals and our family games. We have a tartan of our
own. It is the best. My uncle died, but he lived somewhere else. What
does your father do? How big's your house?

My father drank. My father had a brain. My mother prayed, and then
there was the priest. And we were children: two, three, four, five, six.
My father died and we were not to blame.

We have out family rituals and our family games. Good and better, all
is for the best. My brother drank and he took heroin. The doctors
came. They said he was depressed.

My brother was a baronet. He had no cash. Good and better, bad and
getting worse. My brother died. My brother killed himself. What does
your father do? How big's your house?

129

LOVE POEM

In the bathroom you are cold
   and your nipples
are like dried apricots.
   I hold you back from me,
astonished.

AFTER SHE DROWNED

When she lay there on the table, it was she,
although she was so changed
that no-one who'd not known her as a child
would know her now: the cold skin tight
as a refrigerated peach, the bruises
on her cheek, the long hands strapped
against the upper thighs.
A grey tide had seeped around her forehead
and the hair was matted soft, like moss
or weed. But still she was herself,
that almost smile, her high nose
wrinkled back in slight distaste.
What happened, Kate? What happened? Who was there?
Perhaps she meant to answer, or perhaps
it didn't matter any more. I'd ask around.
I'd find out this and that. Meanwhile,
she lay like someone foundering in sleep,
her winter mouth half open, and the front tooth
glinting like a tiny lamp.
She was nine years old in a fever,
and her torso was bound shut,
a wooden box, containing fragrances.
Her face was tilted to a different sky.
Eyelashes frayed at the edges of her two calm eyes.

2 WREN STREET

It was a moment, sudden as snowflakes,
when the shadow swung luxuriously across the wall
and the elderberries trembled on their fine red stalks.
In the house, a woman sighed in satisfaction and relief

at the white tiles in the ordinary bathroom,
no more washing-up. And it astonished me
to live so comfortably behind my eyes.
Thus it was, in the big room with the pictures
and the crowded shelves, a child was lying softly
on a bed. Orgasms came and went like tiny birds.

Honor Moore

SPUYTEN DUYVIL

The bridge between the Bronx and Manhattan crosses a small body of water
which runs between the Hudson and the East River and is called Spuyten
Duyvil, Dutch for 'the devil's tail'.

1

A computer chip malfunctions. A microscopic switch slips. You cut an apple into

quarters. East of the Urals, a technician
sweats into grey fatigues. In Nevada

a video screen registers activity.
The President carries a briefcase called

the football. His men sit at a small table
or cluster in easy chairs watching a screen

tick with revelation. You adjust your
blinds. I flip a cellar switch. A terrorist

monitors the football. A red light on a red
telephone flashes. The technician cues

his superior. Afternoon in the desert.
Dead of night in the Urals. Rockets

surge from concrete silos like lipsticks sprung
from gargantuan tubes. I have seen bridges

dynamited in 3-D color, mushroom clouds
engorge and shrivel in 4/4 time, faces

of children etched with acid to rippling
wound on screens the size of footballs.

So have you. In a cellar where the ceiling is
low, I bump my head, shatter the only source

of light. This cellar was not built air tight,
but I keep firewood here, my water pump, boiler.

2
I am driving across the bridge
which connects the Bronx to

Manhattan, river blue below, sun
rippling its surprising expanse

and always entering New York
by this route, I love life.

Planes. No, missiles. Or must we
call them warheads? How fast?

Morning: You stand at your kitchen
telephone then drive down the hill.

Or twilight: You bend at a keyboard
moving as you play. Ten minutes

from that place to this. Frozen
expression on the face of

the drunk who wipes my windshield
on the Bowery. I want your

hand. Warheads. You slip an apple,
quarter by quarter, into your mouth.

We never sat facing each other:
What might we make of this love?

3
Anyone who calls a broken heart
a metaphor hasn't seen the crack

in this sunset, fire clouds parting,
cylindrical beasts roaring

toward us. Do they land? Or do objects
tumble blazing, each from an open

hatch? Sudden light so bright
it brings utter darkness. Sound so loud

it could be silence. I am blind and
I step from my car. My hair is

on fire. It could be an earring
or an orange pinwheel. My hand is

burning. My hair stinks when it
burns. Below this bridge at the tip of

the city is a white sand beach. Did you
know that? Tell me, why don't you

reach for my hand? We are all blind, all
feel heat which mounts so fast

I can't tell if I sweat or shiver.

4
My hair has burned back to my
scalp and now my skin is

burning off my brain. Flesh melts
down my leg like syrup. We

won't walk to the river. There's
no mirror and my head is too hot

to touch. The birds are
burning. They say cities will melt

like fat. That one has fewer bones.
Breathe? He was just collecting

our quarters. We were dancing. They
told me this would happen:

Hot oceans, flat darkness.
I stay awake to speak this

My fingers have burned to bone and so
have yours. I never wanted a child,

but I saved everything important
so those who came after could learn.

5
It has not been explained to us that
a computer chip has the shape of

a wafer but is invisible to the
naked eye or that a switch has less

thickness than a capillary or that
the cloud of fire is as fierce and huge as

Niagara Falls. You have chosen
this distance: We will not hear

the terrible news together. When they
tell us we have the power to stop this,

we speak only of our powerlessness
to stop a blizzard in April. There is

nothing more I could have said to you.
You cross the Golden Gate. Planes?

No, missiles. How fast? None of the
children believe they will be

grandparents. Those behind bars will burn
behind bars and I think of flowers. Why

doesn't this scare me as much as losing
love again or not having enough

money? I will break a bone or my bones
will burn. I can't see what's happening

in Nevada. I keep giving them money.
You're not here. My breath

is burning. We must go downstairs, take
hands with the others, speak something.

6
When they said put your head to the wall,
fold your arms behind your neck, I was

not afraid. Even when I saw the movies,
I wasn't afraid, but I am afraid of

burning, of burning and breaking. When
they say we will burn, I feel knives. When

they say buildings will fly apart, that
I will be crushed by a concrete buttress or

a steel beam, I hear the weeping of
everyone into whose eyes I have been

afraid to look. If men carried knives
in airplanes, this is how it would be:

134

Airplanes are silver. They fly across the sky
which is blue. One day a hatch falls open,

knives fly down like rain, and we are all cut
and all bleed. What if, day after day,

knives fell from the sky? I would go into my
cellar, hope my roof would repel knives.

Failure to love has brought us to this.

7
You iron. It could be thunder. They keep
listening to music. Let me tell you, the

difference is the whole city is an
oven which won't go out, and if it could

there would be no one to put it out.
Let me tell you, you will never

see morning again or early spring. Look,
fire sheets down the river like wind

before a hurricane. Listen, it rushes
through city streets like falls down a mountain.

No one will read what you write. No one will
eat what you put on the table. It is not

thunder. There is no time to make amends.
You will not know her as you wished,

and you will never see your face in the
faces of your nieces and nephews.

8
Peel the apple with a knife.
Eat the apple without peeling it.

Choose beautiful paper to draw
her head or draw it on a napkin

after dinner. Eat eggs and sausage
and oranges for breakfast

or don't eat. Drink tea or drink
coffee. Call your father to wish him

happy birthday. Use a bandaid when
you scratch your hand on rose thorn, or

bleed freely into your grandmother's
linen. Plant potatoes as you planned.

Let the candles burn down to stumps
or replace them with new ones.

I have wanted to be free to feel,
to welcome you with flowers,

see your smile time after time.
When the apple limb fell, too heavy

with rain and fruit. I painted its wound
with tar. This year I will fertilize

so the tomatoes have no hardship.
I am not afraid to begin to love or

to keep loving. Even in this fire,
it is not fear I feel but heartbreak.

9
Because he is afraid and powerful
he lives encircled by water.

We hold her as she dies, turn the chairs
to face each other. We breathe with her

as her child is born, let him
cry in the dark as he mourns her death.

When we don't have what we need,
we use what is nearest. One day he

swims the moat to explore the place
which confuses him. There is food when

he reaches the lit house, and stars
hang from the towering branches

of ancient trees. We must learn to rest
when we are tired. Every morning

the sun rises. Every spring green
returns to the cold climates. Bathe

with her, stand with her in her house
smiling as she shows you the

new wood. If their anger frightens you,
try to understand their grief. If you can't

understand what they say, watch
how they move. It's thunder. She

Is young. Tell her the truth. He is near
ninety. Help him cross the street. It's

thunder. Reach for my hand, I will
let you go. It's raining. If you

visit, we will walk down through the fields
and I will show you the river.

CLEIS

She was young. The jeep was yellow. She
cruised past; her style was studied – a white
shirt crisply collared: a visitation, or
an extrapolation, from Sappho's
grove. Invitations had prevented our day
in bed, and we were suffering. Flowers, sun –

we had left brunch. A young woman in a sun
chariot, eyes burning beneath blond bangs, she
drove slowly toward us, a clean car. 'Good day,'
she said. You noted the greeting. The white
pelargonium were still in bloom. Sappho's
girls would be weaving them into garlands, or

dancing, singing what the scent inspired, or
quilling lyres. She leaned out the window, sun
glinting off her tousled brow. Sappho
would have applauded her approach, how she
directed her gaze without guile, whites
of her eyes cossetting blue irises. 'Good day'

was perhaps not all she said. It was Sunday
in California, weather like paradise or
Lesbos, clouds seductively adrift, white
as if to reassert cloud, reflecting sunlight. Our music had begun, our swoon, when she
drove down the hill and hovered. Was she Sappho's

gold-dressed daughter Cleis? Or Sappho's
dapple-throned Aphrodite, girl for a day,
oaring down from heaven in a gold car? She

slowed nonetheless, as if she expected us, or
had perhaps conjured us. We wore sunglasses, so she was not an attack of white

blindness, or any blindness. She was a white-
kirtled vision to tease us back to Sappho's –
dare I speak it? – bower; a trenchant, sun-
drenched mirage to accentuate a day
we were taken transcendentally, or
at least fervently, with one another. She

accelerated. White wheels whirled into day,
and, as Sappho's jeep, emblazoned *NO NUKES OR
WIFE ABUSE* flashed in the sun and vanished, so did she.

Suniti Namjoshi

BIPED

Now that you have hit me,
         I must dab at my mouth
and smile quietly,
         or not smile at all,
but in some way show
         I am noble, not base.
And the dog inside,
         who whimpers
so piteously,
      and would like to lick your hands
– it feels so out of favour –
         that dog must be silenced
before its howling
         betrays disgrace.
But I am that dog.
         It was I who howled,
I who was hurt.
         I felt the pain.
And it is I
      who despised myself.

FROM THE TRAVELS OF GULLIVER
(revised edition)

And I fell in love with a woman so tall that
when I looked at her eyes I had to go star-gazing.

       Tall treasure-houses, moon-
maidenly silence . . . Someday I'll teach you
to smile on me. She sways, sighs,
turns in her sleep. Did a feather fall?
Thor's hammer blow makes no effects.
       I'm told that it's unnatural
to love giantesses.

    In the mornings small dogs bark.
Giantesses strut, fell trees like toothpicks,
while we just stand there, gaze up
their thighs, foreshortened, of course,
but astonishingly pretty.

    One day she picked me up off the floor and set
me on her nipple. I tried to ride, but consider my
position – indubitably tricky.

    To sleep forever in my fair love's arms,
to make of her body my home and habitation . . .
She keeps me about her like a personal worm.
She is not squeamish.

                             Once,
the giddy and gay were gathered together.
Then she brought me out, bathed me
and kissed me. She put me in a suit
of powder blue silk and set me to sail
in a tepid cup of tea. There
I fought out the storm of their laughter.

I performed valiantly.

I love to hear her laugh,
         would not see her grieve,
but a teacup of brine would have seemed
more seemly. I could sail in such a cup,
be swayed by her sighs.

She gluts me on the milk
       of healthy giantesses:

'Poor little mannikin,
              will nothing make you grow?'
I grow. I am growing. You should
                        see me in her dreams.

Nina Newington

POEM FOR JACKIE
One in three women is sexually
abused by the time she is eighteen

you say

              where I was raised
              all the radio played
              all day long
              was the hog reports

              but at night I picked up
              stations
              from Wheeling West Virginia
              Fort Wayne Indiana
              Boston
              that's how I survived

in the town where you were raised
your father raped you
over and over
through all the seasons
until you bled
like a woman

one in three
one in three

my belly like a drum
my fingers beating on a drum
my belly like a drum
my belly like a drum

you say

              I kept it on all night
              turned down low
              I remember the glow of the dial
              green

I was afraid they would laugh at me
for sleeping with the radio on
I didn't sleep

I've seen the skin drawn across your face
so tight I was afraid
it would crack
and bleed

your face like a drum
my belly like a drum

other times your face is like a mask
of copper beaten thin
the art is in the beating
and each blow tells

one in three
one in three

the way you cock your head
is listening
even your eyes are kitten blue
and listening
the lines leading out from them
are maps of places you have heard

you say

> my grandmother
> held me in her lap
> two whole years
> before the war
> ended
> just the three of us
> my mother and my grandmother
> and me
> before the men came home
> I think that gave me the will to fight

your voice   light as a cat
arches into questions
almost every sentence
pauses in between the words

you say

> I used to sit at my grandmother's desk
> with a pencil and a sheet of paper

but the only thing I wrote
was "I want to write"
and sometimes I drew a picture
always the same picture

I can see the pulse
beat
in your throat

turquoise and yellow and red
the clothes you wear now
are plumage for some jungle
where tree clambers tree
and parrots nest in the trunks

you say

for a year I stayed in my room
I painted it black
for eight I took speed every day
my husband never said anything
he liked me to stay home
I guess
I drank every day

so did I
every day
from thirteen on
I tried not to
look back
break any twigs
leave any trace
I ate my own messages
a guerrilla in my own war
on my own ground

swore I would never have children
didn't know why

you say

because I knew I would abuse them

a woman stretched tight as a drum

you listen for my heart beat
when I speak

I was raised in other countries
my father a diplomat
yours a butcher
I fed on other people's worlds
a white in Africa
a child in bed I lay
and listened
for the drums across the water
and footsteps in the hall

it was when my father went away
my mother came for me
over and over
through all the seasons
until I bled
like a woman

she made me make love
to her
which is rape

queer and childless women
we know
you and I
to listen in our bellies
for another beat

in Africa the whites call it
bush telegraph
one drum telling another
the news

I call it
how-we-survive
one in three
one in three
when we survive

my belly like a drum
my fingers beating on a drum
your fingers beating on a drum
your belly like a drum
my belly like a drum
making music from the
inside

other side
other world
hear me
survive

Pat Parker 🖋

WOMANSLAUGHTER

It doesn't hurt as much now –
the thought of you dead
doesn't rip at my innards,
leaves no holes to suck rage.
Now, thoughts of the four
daughters of Buster Cooks,
children, survivors
of Texas Hell, survivors
of soul-searing poverty,
survivors of small town
mentality, survivors,
now three
doesn't hurt as much now.

I
An Act

I used to be fearful
of phone calls in the night –
never in the day.

Death, like the vampire
fears the sun
never in the day –
'Hello Patty'
'Hey big sister
what's happening?
How's the kids?'
'Patty, Jonesy shot Shirley.
She didn't make it.'

Hello, Hello Death
Don't you know it's daytime?
The sun is much too bright today
Hello, Hello Death

you made a mistake
came here too soon, again.
Five months, Death
My sisters and I just met
in celebration of you –
We came, the four strong
daughters of Buster Cooks,
and buried him –
We came the four strong
daughters of Buster Cooks,
and took care of his widow.
We came the four strong
daughters of Buster Cooks
and shook hands with his friends.
We came, the four strong
daughters of Buster Cooks,
and picked the right flowers.
We came, the four strong
daughters of Buster Cooks,
walked tall & celebrated you.
We came, his four strong daughters,
and notified insurance companies,
arranged social security payments,
gathered the sum of his life.

'We must be strong for mother.'

She was the third daughter of Buster Cooks.
I am the fourth.
And in his death we met.
The four years that separated us – gone.
And we talked.
She would divorce the quiet man.
Go back to school – begin again.
Together we would be strong
& take care of Buster's widow.
The poet returned to the family.
The fourth daughter came home.

Hello, Hello Death
What's this you say to me?
Now there are three.
We came, the three sisters
of Shirley Jones,

& took care of her mother.
We picked the right flowers,
contacted insurance companies,
arranged social security payments,
and cremated her.
We came, the three sisters
of Shirley Jones.
We were not strong.
'It is good,' they said,
'that Buster is dead.
He would surely kill
the quiet man.'

II
Justice

There was a quiet man
He married a quiet wife
Together, they lived
a quiet life.

Not so, not so
her sisters said,
the truth comes out
as she lies dead.
He beat her.
He accused her
of awful things
& he beat her.
One day she left.

'Hello, Hello Police
I am a woman
& I am afraid.
My husband means to kill me.'

She went to her sister's house
She, too, was a woman alone.
The quiet man came & beat her.
Both women were afraid.

'Hello, Hello Police
I am a woman
& I am afraid
My husband means to kill me.'

The four strong daughters
of Buster Cooks
came to bury him –
the third one carried a gun.
'Why do you have a gun?'
'For protection – just in case.'
'Can you shoot it?'
'Yes, I have learned well.'

'Hello, Hello Police
I am a woman alone
& I am afraid.
My husband means to kill me.'

'Lady, there's nothing we can do
until he tries to hurt you.
Go to the judge & he will decree
that your husband leaves you be.'
She found an apartment
with a friend.
She would begin
a new life again.
Interlocutory Divorce Decree in hand;
The end of the quiet man.
He came to her home
& he beat her
Both women were afraid.

'Hello, Hello Police
I am a woman alone
& I am afraid
My ex-husband means to kill me.'

'Fear not, lady
He will be sought.'
It was *too* late,
when he was caught.
One day a quiet man
shot his quiet wife
three times in the back.
He shot her friend as well.
His wife died.

The three sisters
of Shirley Jones

came to cremate her –
They were not strong.

III
Somebody's Trial

'It is good,' they said
'that Buster is dead.
He would surely kill
the quiet man.'
I was not at the trial.
I was not needed to testify.
She slept with other men, he said.
No, said her friends.
No, said her sisters.
That is a lie.

She was Black.
You are white.
Why were you there?
We were friends, she said.
I was helping her move
the furniture; the divorce court
had given it to her.
Were you alone? they asked.
No two men came with us.
They were gone with a load.
She slept with women, he said.
No, said her sisters.
No, said her friends.
We were only friends;
That is a lie.
You lived with this woman?
Yes, said her friend.
You slept in the same bed?
Yes, said her friend.
Were you lovers?
No, said her friend.
But you slept in the same bed?
Yes, said her friend.

What shall be done with this man?
Is it a murder of the first degree?
No, said the men,
It is a crime of passion.

He was angry.
Is it a murder of second degree?
Yes, said the men,
but we will not call it that.
We must think of his record.
We will call it manslaughter.
The sentence is the same.
What will we do with this man?
His boss, a white man came.
This is a quiet Black man, he said.
He works well for me
The men sent the quiet
Black man to jail.
He went to work in the day.
He went to jail & slept at night.
In one year, he went home.

IV
Woman-slaughter

'It is good,' they said,
'that Buster is dead.
He would surely kill
the quiet man.'

Sister, I do not understand.
I rage & do not understand.
In Texas, he would be freed.
One Black kills another
One less Black for Texas.
But this is not Texas.
This is California.
The city of angels.
Was his crime so slight?

George Jackson served
years for robbery.
Eldridge Cleaver served
years for rape.
I know of a man in Texas
who is serving 40 years
for possession of marijuana.
Was his crime *so* slight?
What was his crime?
He only killed his wife.

But a divorce I say.
Not final, they say;
Her things were his
including her life.
Men cannot rape their wives.
Men cannot kill their wives.
They passion them to death.

The three sisters
of Shirley Jones
came & cremated her.
& they were not strong.
Hear me now –
It is almost three years
& I am again strong.

I have gained many sisters.
And if one is beaten,
or raped, or killed,
I will not come in mourning black.
I will not pick the right flowers.

I will not celebrate her death
& it will matter not
if she's Black or white –
if she loves women or men.
I will come with my many sisters
and decorate the streets
with the innards of those
brothers in womenslaughter.
No more, can I dull my rage
in alcohol & deference
to *men's* courts.
I will come to my sisters,
not dutiful,
I will come strong.

GROUP

'the primary lesson learned
by any minority is self-hatred'

I do not know
when my lessons began

I have no memory
    of a teacher,
    or books.

osmosis – perhaps
the lessons slip
into my brain,
my cells – silently

I do have memory of
    childhood chants

if you're white – alright
if you're brown – stick around
if you're Black – get back

I do have memory of teachers

you are heathens
why can't you be
like the white kids
you are bad –'

    Bad

& I never thought
to ask the Black teachers
in the all Black schools
How did they know
how white kids were?

    Bad

I do have memory
of playground shouts
'your lips are too big'
a memory of my sisters
putting lipstick
on half of their lips
to make them look smaller

Bad

'your hair is nappy'
I do have memory
of 'Beauty' parlours
& hot combs and grease

Bad

*'stay out of the sun
it'll make you darker'*
I do have memory
of Black & White
bleaching cream
Nadinola
Bleach & Glow

Bad

'your nose is too big'
I do have memory
of mothers pinching
their babies' noses
to make them smaller
Bad
BAD
I do not know
when my lessons
began
do not know
when my lessons
were learned,
absorbed into my cells

now
there are new lessons
new teachers
each week I go to my group
see women
Black women
Beautiful Black Women
& I am in love
with each of them
& this is important
in the loving
in the act of loving

152

each woman
I have learned a new lesson
I have learned
    to love myself

FOR THE STRAIGHT FOLKS
WHO DON'T MIND GAYS
BUT WISH THEY WEREN'T SO BLATANT

you know some people
got a lot of nerve.
sometimes, i don't believe
the things i see and hear.

Have you met the woman
who's shocked by 2 women kissing
& in the same breath,
tells you that she's pregnant?
BUT GAYS SHOULDN'T BE BLATANT.

Or this straight couple
sits next to you in a movie
& you can't hear the dialogue
Cause of the sound effects.
BUT GAYS SHOULDN'T BE BLATANT.

And the woman in your office
Spends your entire lunch hour
talking about her new bikini drawers
& how much her husband likes them.
BUT GAYS SHOULDN'T BE BLATANT.

Or the 'hip' chick in your class,
rattling a mile a minute –
while you're trying to get stoned
in the john
about the camping trip she took
with her musician boyfriend.
BUT GAYS SHOULDN'T BE BLATANT.

You go in a public bathroom
And all over the walls
there's John loves Mary,

Janice digs Richard,
Pepe loves Delores, etc. etc.
BUT GAYS SHOULDN'T BE BLATANT.

Or you go to an amusement park
& there's a tunnel of love
& pictures of straights
painted on the front
& grinning couples
coming in and out.
BUT GAYS SHOULDN'T BE BLATANT.

Fact is, blatant heterosexuals
are all over the place.
Supermarkets, movies, on your job,
in church, in books, on television
every day and night, every place –
even in gay bars.
& they want gay men & women
to go hide in the closets –

So to you straight folks
i say – Sure, i'll go
if you go too,
but i'm polite –
so – after you.

THERE IS A WOMAN IN THIS TOWN

she goes to different bars
sits in the remotest place
watches the other people
drinks till 2 & goes home – alone

some say she is lonely
some say she is an agent
none of us speak to her

Is she our sister?

there is a woman in this town
she lives with her husband
she raises her children

she says she is happy
& is not a women's libber

some say she is misguided
some say she is an enemy
none of us know her

Is she our sister?

there is a woman in this town

she carries a lot of weight
her flesh triples on her frame
she comes to all the dances
dances a lot; goes home – alone

some say she's a lot of fun
some say she is too fat
none of us have loved her

Is she our sister?

there is a woman in this town

she owns her own business
she goes to work in the day
she goes home at night
she does not come to the dances

some say she is a capitalist
some say she has no consciousness
none of us trust her

Is she our sister?

there is a woman in this town

she comes to all the parties
wears the latest men's fashions
calls the women mama
& invites them to her home

some say she's into roles
some say she hates herself
none of us go out with her

Is she our sister?

there is a woman in this town

she was locked up
she comes to many meetings

she volunteers for everything
she crys when she gets upset

some say she makes them nervous
some say she's too pushy
none of us invite her home

Is she our sister?

there is a woman in this town

she fills her veins with dope
goes from house to house to sleep
borrows money wherever she can
she pays it back if she must

some say she is a thief
some say she drains their energy
none of us have trusted her

Is she our sister?

   once upon a time, there was a dream
a dream of women. a dream of women
coming together and turning the world
around. turning the world around and making it over
a dream of women, all women being sisters.
a dream of caring; a dream of protection, a dream
of peace.

once upon a time, there was a dream
a dream of women. for the women who rejected the
dream; there had only been a reassurance. for the
women who believed the dream – there is dying, women,
sisters dying
   once upon a time there was a dream, a dream of women
turning the world all over and it still lives –
it lives for those who would be sisters

it lives for those who need a sister
it lives for those who once upon a time had a dream.

LEGACY

for Anastasia Jean

'Anything handed down from,
or as from an ancestor to a descendant'

PROLOGUE
There are those who think
or perhaps don't think
that children and lesbians
together can't make a family
that we create an extension
of perversion.

They think
or perhaps don't think
that we have different relationships
with our children
that instead of getting up
in the middle of the night
for a 2 a.m. and 6 a.m. feeding
we rise up and chant
'you're gonna be a dyke
you're gonna be a dyke.'

That we feed our children
lavender Similac
and by breathing our air
the children's genitals distort
and they become hermaphrodites.

They ask
'What will you say to them
what will you teach them?'

Child
that would be mine
I bring you my world
and bid it be yours.

Minnie Bruce Pratt

WAULKING SONG: TWO
for C.S.

I

É hó hì ura bhì,
Ho ro ho ì, o ho ro ho.

At first she would not answer
when I asked what was wrong.

Then she told what had happened
in that afternoon when she went to work.

Ho ro ho ì, ó ho ro ho,
É hó hì ura bhì.

Later she gave me the shirt to mend,
a thin K-Mart cotton

with lines of yellow blue and red
running from grey to brighter plaid.

É hó hì ura bhì,
Ho ro ho ì, o ho ro ho.

She had worn it the winter we met.
Under the lines I felt her heart beat.

Many times I had held her and felt
her heart beating beneath that thin cloth.

Ho ro ho ì, ó ho ro ho,
É hó hì ura bhì.

II

Ì u ru rù bhi u o,
Hó í abh o.

In the summer haze she had gone to work.
The man with the knife stopped her.

He shoved her from the door to the straggling hedge.
He jerked at her shirt and ripped the seams.

Chalain éileadh ò hi o,
Ro ho leathag.

158

He cut the buttons off one by one.
He raped her and tried to cut her throat.

He tried to cut her throat. And he did.
The red of her blood crossed the plaid of her shirt.

Ì u ru rù bhi u o,
Hó í abh o.

He asked if she liked it.
When she would not say yes,

He glinted the knife and he laughed.
He laughed and he left. She lay in the dust,

smoked a cigarette, got up,
went home to her trailer, took a bath.

She washed the shirt, put it away,
and looked to see what else was torn.

Chalain éileadh ò hi o,
Ro ho leathag.

III
O ho i o hì ò,
Hao ri o hù ò.

We swore his knife would not part us,
yet fear divided us with many blades.

She did not want me to touch her,
to feel semen and dirt on her skin.

When I moved suddenly, she saw
the sun flash on the knife blade.

She wanted to know where
my hands were at all times.

When I slept with my arm around her,
she dreamed he had her pinned down

and woke night after night saying *no*,
night after night saying *no*.

She feared that I would not touch her,
would not touch, and that I would.

Hao ri o hù ò,
Ro ho i o hì ò.

159

I wanted the red mark to peel
off her throat like a band-aid.

so she would be her self
without this pain: unscarred, unchanged,

not a woman who could have been
dead behind a QuickStop store

a line of ants running from her neck
a woman her friends would not touch.

Ro ho i o hì ò,
O ho i o hì ò.

After three months we wanted her
over it, to be done with dying

while she heard her rape each time
a rock cracked under feet behind her

as she crossed an empty parking lot.
I heard her death each time

a friend spoke the word *rape*
as matter-of-fact as the evening news.

O ho i o hì ò,
Hao ri o hù ò.

That winter, on weekends, when we shared a bed,
we shared bad dreams. We twisted in sheets.

Some nights she heard her voice cry out
and woke herself, breath tearing her throat.

Some nights I felt her shake beside me,
caught in the hedge in December wind.

Before I touched her, I called her name
to wake her before his hand could reach.

We held hands as we talked in the dark.
The shirt lay folded, unmended, in my drawer.

Hao ri o hù ò,
Ro ho i o hì ò.

IV
O ho ì ù ó,
Air fair all ill ó ho.

160

It has been three years; the shirt
was mended, not thrown away.

We rise at dawn to dress for work.
I touch her bare arm. She is alive.

Her heartbeats rush under my fingers.
Her flesh is solid, not cumbled to dust.

Air fair all ill ó ho,
Ro ho hao ri rì ó.

Under my hands, her shoulders spread,
broad, an outcrop of limestone,

under her skin, layers of muscle,
from heft and lift, the weight of her work.

She has made herself strong, enough
to knock a man down, enough

to tell me one night what his hands
had done, the exact, secret wounds.

Ro ho hao ri rì ó,
O ho ì ù ó.

I wanted my hands to be rain for her
to wash away all hurt, the trace of blood.

I did what I could. I took out the shirt,
sewed the buttons back on, one by one,

sewed over each seam, twice, by hand.
He would not ruin what we had made.

O ho ì ú ó,
Air fair all ill ó ho.

She wore the shirt, walked alone to her job.
She would not live in tatters and shreds.

But some afternoons he got his death:
when we heard of a nurse off work, the men,

blackberry vines in an empty lot;
a woman raped at the Gulf station,

stabbed through both eyes with a screwdriver
so she would not see to find him later.

Air fair all ill ó ho,
Ro ho hao ri rì ó.

Then we could not bear witness to our life.
We bought beer and drank to become like stone,

no live woman or dead in our touch.
We cried out with the voice of falling rocks.

We fell asleep, dead weight, in each other's arms,
but always we swore that we would wake up.

Ro ho hao ri rì ó,
O ho ì ù ó.

It has been three years: I wake before dawn
in the dark. I think of the mended shirt.

It still hangs in her closet, the pattern
of red blue yellow lines seamed together.

Her scar has faded to a thin white line.
I can touch her breast. I can feel her heart beating.

He has not ruined what we have made.
At dawn we will rise to dress for work.

O ho ì ù ó,
Air fair all ill ó ho.

V
Hao ri o hù ò,
Ro ho i o hì ò.

When she got to work at five till 8
this morning, a woman named Millie was shot

in the parking lot as she left her car.
The man with the gun watched her blood

disappear into the asphalt. Her boss,
other women watched from a doorway.

At first she asked for help. The man
left to rape a woman in the next street.

In emergency she fought with nurses
who held her to the cart, said *Lie down.*

She said *I know I'm dying. I want*
to sit up. And she did, before she died,

162

while they were saying *Be quiet, you'll be better*.
She was a secretary, three months pregnant.

Ro ho i o hì ò,
O ho i o hì ò.

Do you want me to be quiet? You are tired
of the words *blood, rape, death*.

So am I. I had ended these lines
at the last refrain, but this morning I heard

about Millie. I remembered again your blood
in the dirt, your stomach exposed to the knife.

I want to keep harm from you. I want
to clothe and protect you with my arms.

I look at my hands that held needle and thread.
We resist by whatever means we can.

At work your arm has thrust, your hand
has hefted two feet of steel pipe

over a counter at the man who threatened.
You say *Next time I fight back even if I die*.

Your hands are not quiet; your voice is angry.
I love you because you have refused to die.

O ho i o hì ò,
Hao ri o hù ò.

This poem is for you, to pin to the mended shirt,
like the paper slip you find in a new pocket,

#1949, but you know it's a woman,
all day folding sleeves around cardboard.

At work almost dead on her feet,
she folds the plain thin fabrics.

She thinks of what her hands make at home.
When she leaves the line, the machines are silent.

Her steps make a poem to the rhythm of her heart,
like a poem for you, to pin to the mended shirt.

Hao ri o hù ò,
Ro ho i o hì ò.

163

NOT A GUN, NOT A KNIFE

for C.S.

I don't want this to be happening again, and to you.

Your bruised voice over the phone: *In the bathroom: this
doesn't get easier to say: raped*. And your throat choked
on sperm.
        The words get harder for me to write since the poem
that I gave after your first rape did not work as a lock,

did not bite like a dog when the man shoved
his fingers through your latched screen door and forced
you.
     Of what use this paper of words: not a gun,
not a knife, not the muscle of club by your bed,

not the flimsy surface of my shoulder for you to rest on,
not even the skin of a love letter like those I once wrote you.

But I send it, because this is what I have to give you,
because I know you: smart-handed: can put any scrap to use:

maybe this to be crumpled like kleenex, distraction
or company for your hand if you are crying: maybe

flipped to the blank side for a typed list of curses,
then burned, clean sulphur, ashes fraying:

maybe the page turned to this description: how steadily you
brush at your pale hair in the bathroom, ready to go out

to the bar, talk about nothing much with the women
drinking beer by the pool table, put your quarter down,

twist the blue chalk with tensile fingers against the cue.

Helen Ramsbottom

LESBIANS AND MOTHERS

The pull and tug,
like men with their heels in muddy
earth playing
tug-of-war

164

over your children

the ones I never fathered,
tried to mother,
felt most like an elder sister towards
and played with like a tomboy.

Your kids
hammering a wedge between us
firmly with their small fragile bodies,
                thin as mice

                strong as rocks.

Opposite pain
when they
climb into bed with us;

we bargain over needs,
over Weetabix.

YOUR HAIR, AND

Your hair, and
the ivy you carefully pin to the wall,
blow in the wind outside.

Five storeys up
struggling with an indoor garden,
servicing the plants silently through
holidays, winter frosts, domestic accidents –
changing our council flat from a grey shell
to a green other.

You repot, lug earth
up ten flights; swear at me
for not watering them, watch
their moods, their small
triumphs of a new leaf, a tiny white shoot
in this hostile treeless place.

We spread onto the balcony,
the skyline a battlefield of grey cloud
touching the flats. I
stand watching in the doorway,

your hair, and
the ivy.

BLUE

Blue, blue hyacinth
we fought over you

I bought you for your
Persian blue, your English smell,
purple green sprouting up

I moved you
from room to room,

a trail of dark spring scent

       trickling behind.

Adrienne Rich

IN THE WAKE OF HOME

1
You sleep in a room with bluegreen curtains
posters   a pile of animals on the bed
A woman and a man who love you
and each other   slip the door ajar
you are almost asleep   they crouch in turn
to stroke your hair   you never wake

This happens every night for years.
This never happened.

2
Your lips   steady   never say
It should have been this way
That's not what you say
You   so carefully not asking, *Why?*
Your eyes   looking straight in mine
remind me of a woman's
auburn hair   my mother's hair
but you never saw that hair

The family coil   so twisted, tight and loose
anyone trying to leave
has to strafe the field
burn the premises down

3

The home houses
mirages   memory fogs the kitchen panes
the rush-hour traffic outside
has the same old ebb and flow
Out on the darkening block
somebody calls you home
night after night   then never again
Useless for you to know
they tried to do what they could
before they left for good

4

The voice that used to call you home
has gone off on the wind
beaten into thinnest air
whirling down other streets
or maybe the mouth was burnt to ash
maybe the tongue was torn out
brownlung has stolen the breath
or fear has stolen the breath
maybe under another name
it sings on AM radio:
And if you knew, what would you know?

5

But you will be drawn to places
where generations lie
side by side with each other:
fathers, mothers and children
in the family prayerbook
or the country burying-ground
You will hack your way through the bush
to the Jodensavanne
where the gravestones are black with mould
You will stare at old family albums
with their smiles   their resemblances
You will want to believe that nobody
wandered off   became strange
no woman dropped her baby and ran
no father took off for the hills
no axe splintered the door
— that once at least it was all in order
and nobody came to grief

167

6

Anytime you go back
where absence began
the kitchen faucet sticks in a way you know
you have to pull the basement door
in before drawing the bolt
the last porch-step is still loose
the water from the tap
is the old drink of water
Any time you go back
the familiar underpulse
will start its throbbing: *Home, home!*
and the hole torn and patched over
will gape unseen again

7

Even where love has run thin
the child's soul musters strength
calling on dust-motes   song on the radio
closet-floor of galoshes
stray cat   piles of autumn leaves
whatever comes along
— the rush of purpose to make a life
worth living past abandonment
building the layers up again
over the torn hole   filling in

8

And what of the stern and faithful aunt
the fierce grandmother   the anxious sister
the good teacher   the one
who stood at the crossing when you had to cross
the woman hired to love you
the skeleton who held out a crust
the breaker of rules   the one
who is neither a man nor a woman   the one
who warmed the liquid vein of life
and day after day whatever the need
handed it on to you?
You who did and had to do
so much for yourself   this was done for you
by someone who did what they could
when others left for good

168

9

You imagine an alley   a little kingdom
where the mother tongue is spoken
a village of shelters   woven
or sewn of hides   in a long-ago way
a shanty standing up
at the edge of sharecropped fields
a tenement where life is seized by the teeth
a farm battened down on snowswept plains
a porch with rubber-plant and glider
on a steep city street
You imagine the people would all be there
fathers mothers and children
the ones you were promised would all be there
eating   arguing   working
trying to get on with life
you imagine this used to be
for everyone   everywhere

10

What if I told you your home
is this continent of the homeless
of children sold   taken by force
driven from their mothers' land
killed by their mothers to save from capture
— this continent of changed names and mixed-up blood
of languages tabooed
diasporas unrecorded
undocumented refugees
underground railroads   trails of tears
What if I tell you your home
is this planet of warworn children
women and children standing in line or milling
endlessly calling each others' names
What if I tell you, you are not different
it's the family albums that lie
— will any of this comfort you
and how should this comfort you?

11

The child's soul carries on
in the wake of home
building a complicated house
a tree-house without a tree

finding places for everything
the song   the stray cat   the skeleton
The child's soul musters strength
where the holes were torn
but there are no miracles:
even children become exhausted
And how shall they comfort each other
who have come young to grief?
Who will number the grains of loss
and what would comfort be?

NORTH AMERICAN TIME

I
When my dreams showed signs
of becoming
politically correct
no unruly images
escaping beyond borders
when walking in the street I found my
themes cut out for me
knew what I would not report
for fear of enemies' usage
then I began to wonder

II
Everything we write
will be used against us
or against those we love.
These are the terms,
take them or leave them.
Poetry never stood a chance
of standing outside history.
One line typed twenty years ago
can be blazed on a wall in spray paint
to glorify art as detachment
or torture of those we
did not love but also
did not want to kill

We move   but our words stand

170

become responsible
for more than we intended

and this is verbal privilege

III
Try sitting at a typewriter
one calm summer evening
at a table by a window
in the country, try pretending
your time does not exist
that you are simply you
that the imagination simply strays
like a great moth, unintentional
try telling yourself
you are not accountable
to the life of your tribe
the breath of your planet

IV
It doesn't matter what you think.
Words are found responsible
all you can do is choose them
or choose
to remain silent.   Or, you never had a choice,
which is why the words that do stand
are responsible

and this is verbal privilege

V
Suppose you want to write
of a woman braiding
another woman's hair –
straight down, or with beads and shells
in three-strand plaits or corn-rows –
you had better know the thickness
the length   the pattern
why she decides to braid her hair
how it is done to her

what country it happens in
what else happens in that country

You have to know these things

171

VI

Poet, sister: words –
whether we like it or not –
stand in a time of their own.
No use protesting   *I wrote that*
before Kollontai was exiled
Rosa Luxemburg, Malcolm,
Anna Mae Aquash, murdered,
before Treblinka, Birkenau,
Hiroshima, before Sharpeville,
Biafra, Bangladesh, Boston,
Atlanta, Soweto, Beirut, Assam
– those faces, names of places
sheared from the almanac
of North American time

VII

I am thinking this in a country
where words are stolen out of mouths
as bread is stolen out of mouths
where poets don't go to jail
for being poets, but for being
dark-skinned, female, poor.
I am writing this in a time
when anything we write
can be used against those we love
where the context is never given
though we try to explain, over and over
For the sake of poetry at least
I need to know these things

VIII

Sometimes, gliding at night
in a plane over New York City
I have felt like some messenger
called to enter, called to engage
this field of light and darkness.
A grandiose idea, born of flying.
But underneath the grandiose idea
is the thought that what I must engage
after the plane has raged onto the tarmac
after climbing my old stairs, sitting down
at my old window
is meant to break my heart and reduce me to silence.

172

IX
In North America time stumbles on
without moving, only releasing
a certain North American pain.
Julia de Burgos wrote:
That my grandfather was a slave
is my grief: had he been a master
that would have been my shame.
A poet's words, hung over a door
in North America, in the year
nineteen-eighty-three.
The almost-full moon rises
timelessly speaking of change
out of the Bronx, the Harlem River
the drowned towns of the Quabbin
the pilfered burial mounds
the toxic swamps, the testing-grounds

and I start to speak again

TRACKING POEMS

(The following poems are part of a longer
sequence. The original numerical notation
has been retained.)

1
Look: this is January   the worst onslaught
is ahead of us   Don't be lured
by these soft grey afternoons   these sunsets cut
from pink and violet tissue-paper   by the thought
the days are lengthening
Don't let the solstice fool you:
our lives will always be
a stew of contradictions
the worst moment of winter can come in April
when the peepers are stubbornly still   and our bodies
plod on without conviction
and our thoughts cramp down before the sheer
arsenal of everything that tries us:
this battering, blunt-edged life

173

2

Heart of cold. Bones of cold. Scalp of cold.
the grey the black the blond the red
hairs on a skull of cold. Within that skull
the thought of war the sovereign thought
the coldest of all thought. Dreaming shut down
everything kneeling down to cold intelligence
smirking with cold memory
squashed and frozen cold breath
half held-in for cold. The freezing people
of a freezing nation eating
luxury food or garbage
frozen tongues licking the luxury meat
or the pizza-crust the frozen eyes
welded to other eyes also frozen
the cold hands trying to stroke the coldest sex.
Heart of cold Sex of cold Intelligence of cold
My country wedged fast in history
stuck in the ice

3

My mouth hovers across your breasts
in the short grey winter afternoon
in this bed we are delicate
and tough so hot with joy we amaze ourselves
tough and delicate we play rings
around each other our daytime candle burns
with its peculiar light and if the snow
begins to fall outside filling the branches
and if the night falls without announcement
these are the pleasures of winter
sudden, wild and delicate your fingers
exact my tongue exact at the same moment
stopping to laugh at a joke
my love hot on your scent on the cusp of winter

6

Dear Adrienne:
       I'm calling you up tonight
as I might call up a friend as I might call up a ghost
to ask what you intend to do
with the rest of your life. Sometimes you act
as if you have all the time there is.
I worry about you when I see this.

174

The prime of life, old age
aren't what they used to be;
making a good death isn't either,
now you can walk around the corner of a wall
and see a light
that already has blown your past away.
Somewhere in Boston   beautiful literature
is being read around the clock
by writers   to signify
their dislike of this.
I hope you've got something in mind.
I hope you have some idea
about the rest of your life.

In sisterhood,

Adrienne

7

Dear Adrienne,
                    I feel signified by pain
from my breastbone through my left shoulder down
through my elbow into my wrist is a thread of pain
I am typing this instead of writing by hand
because my wrist on the right side
blooms and rushes with pain
like a neon bulb
You ask me how I'm going to live
the rest of my life
Well, nothing is predictable with pain
Did the old poets write of this?
– in its odd spaces, free,
many have sung and battled –
But I'm already living the rest of my life
not under conditions of my choosing
wired   into pain

rider on the slow train

Yours, Adrienne

8

I'm afraid of prison. Have been all these years.
Afraid they'll take my aspirin away
and of other things as well:
beatings   damp and cold   I have my fears.
Unable one day to get up and walk

175

to do what must be done
Prison as idea   it fills me
with fear   this exposure to my own weakness
at someone else's whim
I watched that woman go over the barbed-wire fence
at the peace encampment
                              the wheelchair rider
I didn't want to do what she did
I thought, They'll get her for this
I thought, We are not such victims.

13
Trapped in one idea, you can't have your feelings,
feelings are always about more than one thing.
You drag yourself back home and it is autumn
you can't concentrate, you can't lie on the couch
so you drive yourself for hours on the quiet roads
crying at the wheel   watching the colors
deepening, fading   and winter is coming
and you long for one idea
one simple, huge idea to take this weight
and you know you will never find it, never
because you don't want to find it
You will drive and cry and come home and eat
and listen to the news
and slowly even at winter's edge
the feelings come back in their shapes
and colors   conflicting   they come back
   they are changed

18
The problem, unstated till now, is how
to live in a damaged body
in a world where pain is meant to be gagged
uncured   un-grieved-over   The problem is
to connect, without hysteria, the pain
of any one's body with the pain of the body's world
For it is the body's world
they are trying to destroy forever
The best world is the body's world
filled with creatures   filled with dread
misshapen so   yet the best we have
our raft among the abstract worlds

176

and how I longed to live on this earth
walking her boundaries   never counting the cost

19
If to feel is to be unreliable
don't listen to us
if to be in pain is to be predictable
embittered   bullying
then don't listen to us
If we're in danger of mistaking
our personal trouble for the pain on the streets
don't listen to us
if my fury at being grounded frightens you
take off on your racing skis
in your beautiful tinted masks
Trapped in one idea, you can't have feelings
Without feelings perhaps you can feel like a god

Jennifer Rose 🖎

AT DACHAU WITH A GERMAN LOVER

I won't go with you to Munich's planetarium
though I have always loved a wandering moon.
I cannot bear to bless a German heaven.

Dachau. The sign appears, colloquial
amidst the traffic; the radio sputters
stau – or is it *heil*?

Everything continues in this language!
Every chimney rises with a grudge.
The *Arbeit* gate swings slowly on its hinge.

This is the first time I feel at home
in your country, in this museum.
Elsewhere, the Nazis are innocuous, your neighbors.

You examine by yourself their careful orders.
Every road to death is neatly chartered.
You're horrified – not just by deaths of strangers,

but by the language, which killed them

before the gas or gunners;
your language, words you might have uttered.

Tell me what it says, this chart of stars:
Which color is my destiny of fire –
yellow, for the language of my prayers?

red, for the fury of my cares?
or pink, my crime of twin desires?
This is my planetarium, these pinned-on stars!

You won't go with me to Dachau's crematorium
though the ovens are cold, the fumes are gone,
and you're too young to have fired them.

The gas chamber, familiar as a dream
but smaller, is open at both ends.
I walk, without knees, without lungs, the brief

avenue. This is it. The vault, the safe
where they escaped, scratching
in the old direction of heaven.

At night our room is dark, the bed, a ditch.
The moon grows big in its hutch as we watch,
wide awake, tense. Your father was a soldier,

your mother, a Hitler youth who quit.
I'm a Jew. I'd be dead if we were older.
What shocked me most as we first slowed

to stop was not Dachau's walls or weight,
but its shamelessness at its own sight.
Had no one seen the guards guarding their flawed height,

the smoke drifting off, signalling in desperate code?
This is what I can't forget:
how public it was, how close to the road.

Barbara Ruth

FAMILIAL AMNESIA

You ask me how my family
Celebrates the holidays.
The holidays?

To my Mom and Dad that means Christmas
Thanksgiving
Easter
And they celebrate them
As their neighbors do
Nothing distinctive
Nothing to call attention to themselves
They do not remember
What holidays they used to celebrate
What candles lit
What drums beat
In their childhood homes.
They have forgotten the prayers
Do not name the languages
The dates
Printed in red
On the Christian calendar
Are all that they observe.

You ask me about heritage
What I remember from my childhood.
I recall
Watching what the others did
Imitating classmates, teachers
Learning to ridicule my grandparents
For their food, their accents
The things that made them stand out
The things that made them foreign.

My mother
Mispronounces what few Yiddish words
She remembers
My father
Does not know (or will not say)
His clan affiliations.

My parents think
Forgetting will protect them
'It was all so long ago'
'That's not the way we live now'

Sometimes I pretend
We are *conversos*
Secretly observing my holy days
In a hidden basement

Only some of us know exists
I search the lower levels
Press against the walls
Hoping one will be a panel
Which turned into a door
Leading to the *kiva*
To the *seder* table
Where the pipe, the *afikomen*
Have been safekept all these years
Waiting
For someone to remember.

Sapphire

SOME THINGS ABOUT THE POLITICS OF SIZE

1
Big women git ignored
or stared at
or people look away and try not to see
big women get more than their share of
disdain, ridicule
the bigger you are
the less you're seen
they cant take their eyes off the rolls of flesh
the lumps, hanging belly
the fat compels tears out their eyes
but you remain invisible
fat and ugly become synonymous
you can be ugly without being fat
but you cant be fat without being ugly
and in the land of the beautiful
to be ugly is to be unseen
like being differently formed, no one can take their eyes off
the missing or different limb, in this case the, to their mind,
    excess flesh
admission of greasy lip nites, secret masturbatory glory
swathed in chocolate, grits, fried things and cream puffs that
turn to ripples on your thighs, hard lumps on your hips,
mountains of flesh out of control out of control
seeping over elastic waistbands, spilling from underneath bras

forming hills that sit on thighs sweet sweet looking for
something to eat, round defiance, corpulent rebellion
in the land of Farah Fawcett and Jackie O so slim so rich
   so wite
in the land of the free and the slave
in the land of the never too thin never too rich
to be big is to be invisible
the wider the you, the narrower the view

2
When you are big cute cloze dont fit
you wear big blouses from India
little boys will call you fatso
a total stranger walked past me and said smoothly
chilling me, 'You're getting fatter.' The reason blunted
the assault sharp.
You can be exercising your human right to eat a donut
when and where you choose, such as walking down the street
and at the same time choose not to respond to some
teenagers, 'Hey Baby,' as you eat and be told, 'That's why you fat!'
No thot, compunction – you are the butt of insult, you are a joke
fat joke fat joke fat joke laff laff till you cry vomit laff laff
at yor big ass your funny rotund gigantic ass everyone knows
you eat too much weight weight better get that weight off if
you wanna dance act sing. Sing? What singing got to do with fat?
Ask Florence Ballard and Dinah Washington.
Drop drop the pounds the pills till your mouth dry up and your brain
burns a marathon in circles dry you up wasted your mind nerves
gain back more than you ever lost fast fast at last 14 day fast enema
colonic fast plastic pants sweat sweat the fat is still there
it is the last to go sweat sweat water heart tissue, muscle tissue,
brain tissue go first, too weak now to wear the pretty dress or
running shorts, too tired to show off the cellulite free legs
Ahh some green and orange dexadrine left at the bottom of the
tiny amber vial, now we feel good like a cigarette should puff
puff ANYTHING rather than eat, leave your money at home
dont bring it you might buy something to eat
oh god oh god i'm gonna kill myself i cant stand it ugh!
i hate looking in the mirror
if i wasnt so fat i'd be – i'd do – i could – if i wasnt so fat
i would – as soon as i lose weight i'm gonna . . .

3
There was a lady who got so fat that when she got sick

181

and had to go to the hospital they had to get the fire department
to knock the walls of her house out cause she couldnt fit out the door.
I read that in *Jet Magazine*. How did she get to the bathroom – take a
bath, piss, shit? The light of day? How long had she gone without a
    walk
to the store, church? How did she live? Even welfare demands a
face to face every three months. Did she have a husband, lover?
500 lbs. That's deep. They had a picture of them bringing her out.
It took a lot of them. She looked blurred, a dark mountain with short
pressed hair sticking up.
(now for some reason sitting here retyping this I think of the goddess.)

4
Dexatrim, Metracal, Pepsi Light, Diet Pepsi, Diet 7UP, No Cal, Lo
Cal devoid of sugar fulla chemicals saccharin, cyclamates,
dexadrine, dexamil, benzadrine take a pill DexatrimMetracal
PepsiLightDietPepsi7UPNoCalLoCaldevoidofsugarfullachemicals
saccharincyclamatesdexadrinedexamilbenzadrinetakeapill
dexatrimmetracalpepsilightdietpepsi7upnocallocaldevoidofsugar
fullachemicalssaccharincyclamatesdexadrinedexamilbenzadrine
takeapillpillpill

5
Fat people dont suffer. The lithe and pale pine away.
Surrounded by flesh equals insensitive. Yes, of course,
if you were sensitive you wouldnt be fat. But anyway,
the maiden by the sea has long brown hair, anemic skin, her eyes
are deep dark burning wells with smokey circles underneath,
the anguish of unrequited love eats away at her, her skin stretches
over protruding cheek bones.
The maid the maid she sleeps on old sheets under a worn coverlet.
Suet, blood porridge, her cheeks as apples, rolls around her waist
like large wite donuts *dull* insentient creature that has never
known upper class heart rendering appetite killing love.
The slave the slave she is lacing Scarlett O'Hara into her stays.
Little southern sylph. Fat black elephant. Ponderous lump of lard
devoid of any emotion except worry, worry over her everloving
in love PASSIONATE winsome, long haired, thin, mistress, 'Oh
    Missy!
you gone kill yourself, you got me worried near bout to death! You ain
et, you ain slept, come on wont you please eat a little somethin for
    Mammy!'
Where her thighs meet are sore now, the flesh rubbing together has
chafed the skin. The bright wite shoulder straps of the 48EEE bra cut

deep into hcr flcsh, the whalebone is a constant hurt girdling the fat,
keeping it in, from jiggling. She is strong standing over the stove,
ironing cloze, starched, crisp, unsmelling, unfucked. Now she is totally
for them, who jump on her bosom finding familiarity and reassurance
    in the
soft mammoth, a comfort, they wouldnt have her any other way.

6
meso
ecto
endo
MORPH
hard & muscular
tall & thin
soft & round
which are you?
which would you rather be?
ecto
endo
ecto
meso
MORPH

7
Fat people are hated.
'. . . work has been done to delineate the ways in which these body
types are perceived by others on the basis of shared cultural beliefs.
. . . the endomorph (rounded) body type was clearly seen as
    perjorative.
The endomorph was described with words like lazy, mean, and dirty,
    while
such words as strong, friendly, healthy, and brave were used to
    describe the
mesomorph.
. . . this was believed in general by all people (fat, thin, or athletic)
it was found that wite male and female school children wished to and
did keep greater distance from the endomorph than the other two
    body types.
. . . Dyrenforth, Freeman and Wooley examined the attitudes of *pre-
    school age*
[emphasis mine] children in an effort to find the age at which such
    concepts

emerge. When presented with two life-size rag dolls, identical in every
   way except corpulence 91% of the children who expressed a
   preference indicated
they preferred the thin doll over the fat doll . . . it was striking to note
that although three of the overweight children correctly identified
themselves as being 'like' the fat doll, all three preferred the thin doll.
. . . obese high school seniors were found to be accepted for college
   admission
less often than normal-weight girls.
The obese were less likely to be helped out by strangers than the
   normal-
weight people.'*
did ya hear what I said? i said: FAT PEOPLE ARE HATED.

* 'A Woman's Body in a Man's World: A Review of Findings on Body Image and
Weight Control' by Susan Dyrenforth, Orlando W. Wooley, Susan C. Wooley from
A Woman's Conflict: A Special Relationship between Women and Food, Jane Rachel
Kaplan (ed), Prentice Hall Inc., New Jersey, 1980.

I GUESS IF I WAS A SOUND
OR
IF I WAS YOUR WOMAN

i guess if i was a sound
i'd be a saxophone
a drumbeat
ocean wave
heart beat and if i was something to eat
i'd be an eggplant
mango strawberry
blackberry banana
pear raspberry
luv juice orange
blk beans brown rice and if i was something to wear
i'd be red silk
clean cotton
fine wool
i'd be a hi heeled trumpet
gold ring warrior
with a feather shield
an opium dream
a real wind storm

soft sea
i'd be banana bread
and chocolate lips
thighs clenched around
your hips
a lightning flash on
your clitoris
i would be cinnamon
tea tears soft
smiles   smooth skin
hot bath
attentive woman
i would be warm things
and wash your feet
i would be a communion
a union of love need
green things growing
in your mind
if i was a touch
i'd be fur on a cat's back
burlap   a silk sand
hot wet thing
if i was a sight i'd be
an African print gold hoop
brown round glorious
red bird   a mirage
of mad things
if i was a smell
i'd be sesame oil
coconut natural
funky thing
i'd be flowers
and sweat
perfume and piss
manufactured and
real   i'd be a sweet
thing open
wide to your need
a bowl a river
to flow fill
i'd be black ink
grey fears
midnite madness

and if i was a jewel
i'd be a Rubylee Pearl Sapphire Opal
Crystal girl and
if i was machine
i'd break down
decompose and
go back to the
earth
'i'd never stop lovin
loving you
i'd never stop
loving you
i say i say I SAY
i'd never stop
loving you.'

Susan Sherman

A FARE/WELL PRESENT

Well   good-bye
and all that means
if in fact it means
anything
                        words sometimes
taking the place
of meaning
                        like last night
twisted in my own
syllables   trying
to explain

Or that summer
seven years old
first time away from home
A feeling of the heart
but literally that

                        The camp director
calling it 'homesick'
or 'missing'
Not only that something
was missing

                    that I was missing
someplace or someone
but that somehow
I was also missing
from something   somewhere
I wanted to be

A seven-year-old pride
denied it denies it still
but now with how much more vehemence
command of language
skill with words
                         no longer only
(shoulders out   chest squared)
'homesick   not *me*'
but paragraphs of explanation
reams of words
                         to say only
somewhere something
has been left out
is out of place

And so   as a farewell present
I give you this poem
This feeling of the heart
That when I think of you
leaving

            And when I think of you here
and can't be with you
Even when we are together
when I feel you growing distant
I experience that
                         'missing'
that something
left out
as if I am discovering the word again
for the first time
What it really means

As with all things that move us
deeply
                the feeling comes
                                     first
the experience

As we perceive the meaning
The word
                    follows later
'missing'

that space which is not empty
but fills all space

Linda Smukler

HE TOUCHED ME

He touched me and the shivery circle came around my head   he
touched me and my eyes went out   out   pretty girl   out   he
touched me and my belly skin got small   my back skin crawled
away   he touched me   black hair   he touched me and I couldn't
breathe   if I sucked the air the ants would come back to my ribs   I'd
turn inside out and shrivel up   he crawled down on my belly   what
are you?   He reached down to my toes   three little piggies   there
was a song in my ears   low auouu like a hundred cows   he touched
me and the scent of burning took me up in the air   up and I couldn't
see anymore   couldn't hear   He touched me and the rush of me
rushed out and I got knocked through the air   Charles come on –
she should be asleep by now   mom was at the door   from the
ceiling I saw him reach over my head   he closed the bambi book and
put out the light   he kissed my forehead   good night he said   and
got up   the bed sprung up to catch me as he went out the door   I
sighed and breathed back into myself   I felt lighter than air and the
ghost blue nightlight floating in the dark   there was wind outside   I
heard it as the cows died in my ears

MONKEY BOY

I lift my hand to my face   my hand's the biggest thing around and
filled with rivers   it has stems I can see through to the dark fuzzy
air   I hold my hand to my face and down below I feel my legs curl up
to my chest   I look out at the door of my room   it's open a crack
and there's light   it's pink and dim   night light they say   light
for daddy to see when he comes in the crack   light for me to not be
afraid   monkey's here too   I can feel his hard face and his big ears
and the straps that hold up his checkered pants   his name is Jim and

he sleeps with me every night   he's here when I'm naked   he's here
when I open my eyes and my stomach hurts and the bed is wet   he's
here when I'm high up on a pole stuck right up through me and people
are laughing and I can't get down   he's here and he runs on his hard
curly toes and takes me away   like he'll go and get somewhere like
Wyoming where I can jump into his body and be there too   in
Wyoming my name is Ace   Jim Ace the monkey boy who can run
forever and climb the tallest trees   whose hair is dark and whose
eyes can see rattlesnakes a mile away   who has no mother or father
and lives fine by himself   Jim Ace the monkey boy sleeps under the
stars where the light is blue and green and there are sometimes wolves
but the wolves are his friends   they sing to him hello Jim Ace across
the plains   hello Jim Ace   my ears have grown larger than
monkey's ears   hello I shout back across the plains   then the night
floats down and the wolves come close and lie in a circle around
me   where I am the center and I sleep

Kay Stirling

ONE NUTMEG WITH ITS COAT OF MACE

Myristica Fragrans produces two
separate spices – from the box
of a West Indian nutmeg

i

> Matsumet oranges from Spain
> apricots from the Middle East
> nutmeg in its home of mace
>
> figs   figs   figs

Can we call this Christmas?

No pudding, no pie, no
white meat, grace
the table.
>   At the centre of our shared surface –
the nutmeg
>   rocks, rolls
in its shell.

The mace encloses the shell.
The shell encases the nutmeg.

Fingers of mace
curl, wrap, contain
                    the nut
                    the heart

ii
Beyond protective windows, wind
howls, whips branches
from trees; trips slates
from the roof, the heart's ceiling
the ceiling's limit.

                                        Drip

                                    drip

                                        drip

till the bucket is full
the basin
the bowl
        – all overflow

The bedroom is adrift; the bed
still ten feet off the floor
is teetering on stilts.
Water rises.
                    This *could* be Bangkok or Bali . . .
                    in 'the wet', but not
The Bible.
Not seven days, not seven nights.
This is not Christmas.
This is not Noah and his knowable
flood.

                    We are on our own.
                    Our mission . . .?
to sink, or
swim.

iii
We make forays downstairs
for small amounts of food.
The water follows us

rapids down the stairs
seepings under the sills.

Newspapers, old stockings, toilet paper
cannot contain it.

Snot flows freely
down the face.

This is Xmas

the artificial lights
the pine needles.

We manage a little raw fish,
blink back salt,
sink into tenderness;
drown
      again
          and again.

Words punctuate
      puncture

How much imagination?
      effort?
How many holes . . .
            can we conceive
                    stop up
                      keep up
to the point of painful birth?

The waters breaking.
The tide returning.

No walking on water.
No delusions.
No parting of the waves.

A parting of the ways?
A cross-road?
A murderous highway?

            Intersection.

            Intersection.

We can't leave;
the storm outside is a killer
the whale will swallow us whole.
There's no argument.

We are not Jonah,
cannot be spat out, intact.

We remain in the eye
of the storm, the infinite water
the ocean, the sea of ourselves

iv
Cradle me! Cradle me!
Don't tip me out yet.

> *When I was a young girl*
> *I'd never been kissed . . .*
>
> *Oh . . . oh . . . oh kisses*
> *sweeter than wine*
>
> *Drink to me only with thine eyes*
> *and I will . . .*
> > *water water everywhere*
> *and not a drop . . .*
>
> *There's a hole in the bucket*
> *Dear Liza, dear Liza*
> *There's a hole in the bucket*
> *Dear Liza,*
> > *a hole*
> *Then fix it . . .*
>
> *My eyes are dim*
> *I cannot see*
> *I have not brought my specs with me*
> *I have not brought my specs with me . .*

I need time
clarity
        to unravel
        re-negotiate

– When does a rhyme become repetitive?

– In what era does allegory spell tall story?

Underneath myth,
                chapter and verse
lies plucked tongue
    buttoned lip
    damned tears

Give me a myth
and I will give you a penny
for your thoughts
and nothing
for your feelings
                    just
touch me
          simply
                    touch . . .

                    Help, I need somebody
                    Help, not just anybody

v
Cradle me! Cradle me!
Don't tip me out, yet.

Watch out for the bough breaker,
the wanker, the ones
that will call us the ball breakers –

Have we lived long enough
to detect an eye for an eye?
tooth for tooth?
The difference? The danger?

Give me all your eyes, your teeth
your extravagant heart, and
I will consider
how much of me
I am prepared
to have nibbled . . .
                    my nose
                    my lobes
                    my webbed toes

come into me
        into me

                    Give me all your love
                    all your love

        enough is
        enough
                is . . .

I want you
I want you to want me all up

193

I want you to keep your distance
I want you to want distance

Don't stay over there, the other end
of the settee;
it's too far.

                  I'm submerging
hold me
keep me
        up

The nutmeg is inside.
The mace hugs the shell.
Fingers curl, wrap, contain

                      the nut
                      the nub

vi

        Snap fingers

        of mace

        containing the shell

        Smash the shell

        enclosing the kernel

        Grate the heart

        for the spice

vii
This is Christmas colliding
into New Year
through the eye
of the needle, the eye
of the storm

      I, you, me, you

The deluge
     us
        the difficult heart

of the matter
        breaking
free
of miracles

C. Linden Thorp

WE FEED OURSELVES

Suck
pull through teeth
imagined milk
like orgasm
sort solids from
non-solids

gravitated
to taste your nipple
there   ready
sheer

gripped
the body-bud filled
of purple flesh
pinched with arabesque fingers
the stopper on Dutch cheese

through
the funnel of your mother
I here at you
as you at her
House of Women

pulled
you outside
as you tugged
in intelligent teeth
the woman-child at tether
no blood-spill

glut
rip your organ
tear   draw
pull up its pistil
sinew-soft   bite

Hush.

scoop
my intent head
push me down you

to lap thick-coming
womb-milk

We feed ourselves from
ancient reservoirs

NOT FOR YOU

This life beneath ice
is not for you, my darling,
this cold rank fever of isolation,
its torment of dislocations,
not for you, my desperate child.
This frosted visibility, thickened,
its smoothness utter, lethal,
is not for your warm fingers to
slip on as you press and push,
not for you to incur scratches and burn.
Not for you, my once-happy girl.

You come here beneath on the
rope-bridge of a kiss
where I feed you iced spoons of my vision,
a few drops of my sparse happiness to taste.
This life of mine is not for you,
my sweet mammalian woman.

THE ORGASM

She, insect, climbs the
glass bosom of love,
bickers down the side,
and, fully repaired,
climbs again.

She, in her container,
is held in sweaty hands,
clasped by her love-master,
and is shaken hard,
a hard dice.

She rattles,
some hardness knocks

some fleshiness.
Her yelps of nutmeg
are absent of child.

She, aeons before,
supine on a modern duvet,
beckoned with redolence.
Now she shuns
like a trapped moth.

She has no quills,
just bread-fruit front,
where milk-jewel clitoris
leads to clotted birth-yard
And there she pins her inquiline.

Lisa Vice

SLEEPING WITH MEN

I found out where meat came from
and didn't want to eat it
my mother said
you need it to live
and I couldn't leave the table until my plate was clean.
I swore I'd sit there
until hell froze over
but succumbed in the end
gagging on the cold gristle and bone.

WHO ELSE YOU GOT?

Yesterday
I heard you humming
the song we sang when you still wanted to sit on my lap

Now you're upstairs with the door shut
in this heat
it's that boy again   that boy again
cool talk sweet smoke you give it all away
forget
your father isn't even a photograph

I kneel by the window
fingernails scratching onto a granite headstone
I could not be
mommy/daddy/auntie/uncle/sister/brother/grammy/grampy/
soul provider
friendofthefamily/armysergeant/allloving/allforgiving/
always there for you

Honey
I carried you long after my shoulders began to ache
never able to put you down
say   here
feel the pressure ease
in that place where the skull meets the spine
even after you walked and talked
tied your shoes
read and wrote

Sometimes I slammed you down
hands smacking your back
the only thing that felt good

did we drown together long ago
in soggy diapers/diarrhoea/black walled rooms
welfare checks   lost or stolen
birthday cards   never received

locked together
fingernail to wrist
I hear my mother's voice
who else you got?
slamming my foot in the door
who else cares about you?

could I have left you
barefoot on the subway
shuffling through cellophane and newspapers
dreaming of a dime, a bagel, a room with a door?

if I could
I would go back
suck the bruises from your bones like a bloated leech
shrivel and shrink under our salt

DOROTHY

Dorothy knew how to have a good time
at the Backlash
evening in paris
dabbed behind each ear
drank highballs
didn't give a damn about the hickey on her neck
lived proud
in that flat dinky town
head high
white heels clicking through sawdust
in Raleigh Freeman's grocery

everybody knew

she lived on Winstons
black coffee
dark haired men
dancing with them to the car radio
on dead end roads
leaving red tipped butts
in their ashtrays
souvenirs for their wives

what did she care

her womb gone already
her teeth too
cysts on her ovaries
cysts on her breasts
ulcers bleeding into her stomach

hell

SISTERS

remember when
the new sears roebuck catalogue came
the old one ours at last
shiny pages memorized
frozen faces long named and claimed

rainy days spent
cutting out women

in pedal pushers
women
in plaid pleated skirts
you wanted the blonde with the missing hand
I wanted the brunette in a quilted robe
on the other side of the page

we spread them all over
the red faded living room rug
gave our women washing machines
husbands
new sheets
smiling children
in clean new clothes
white plates
with golden sheaves of wheat

Linda,
you grew up
before I was ready
left me
on the floor
with a sack of paper lives

Marg Yeo

LEAVES AND POTATOES

my friend is a thin
woman   eating
potatoes
                5 or
6 at once
and keeps extra
teeth in a
cup in the kitchen for
emergencies

she is very
leafy
                i have never known any
one so
leafy as she

is
   with her   in
side is very much like out
side   only with
furniture in it

when i think
of her   it is
thin   but
solid and potato
simple
        and sudden with leaves in
side and
everywhere

THE TRUTH OF IT

i
i'm raw   like a scraped
knee but all over   and inside
too
     it's not surprising that i bleed
sporadically   or too much   or
not at all   that i feel i
might explode
         shell gone
suddenly i'm all over everyone   and it's
embarrassing   i'm not
used to it   i am my
own woman
        and afraid of
growing old

that's the truth of it

there's never enough
time
     i'm not done with anything and ready
for the next bit before it's here and
gone again and i'm scraping the bits
up and pasting them together as i run to catch
up with a woman (who is probably
myself) just out of

sight   out of my
reach   ahead

who knows where she's
heading   i haven't figured it out   not even after all
these years

i have no
answers   and i am
angry about it   intolerant   testy   *i am a hard
woman* i tell everyone and they
believe me

o i am a soft woman and sticky like
treacle i
melt on the tongue

everything about me contradicts
me   i am too much of this and
that and the next thing to
ever be whole   a scrapbag patchwork worn too
thin

(but it's poems and
women wrap my thin
skin in)

ii
it's poems and
women wrap my thin
skin in
        grow whole and
line by line and
limb by limb delight
me

i see
        a woman nursing a child in a back
garden full of women where a woman
reads her poems out of sight of the distant
roar of the street among
flowers (it is something
religious   a common
spirit here and for this
hour at least   nothing can
touch us)

i see
        a poet
signing her book for a woman whose baby
drowses against her (who asks for both
names   hers and the child's
                        *her first
reading* she says *so she'll
remember*)

*it's a hard
world* you say *so what hope is
there?*

all i
know are the ragtag and bobtail
of keepsakes
                a tangle of
words fingers   the breath of this
woman or that one soft along my
cheek   the ache of
silence and the fine
delight there is
                will always
be   for me   in
poems and women

SHE GREW WHOLE
for wend

i
she grew whole   someone
said   like a rose
                    stem   leaf   bud and
petal in their natural order and
perfect   nothing to
twist her out of shape

she must have come
to in a tight steamy
greenhouse and grown straight
up   no storm tearing her   no
wind wearing her away

but no
bee brought a message and
kissed her with it

no creature trudged the
acres of her stem and settled
in intimate
            no one clutched and
clung and bled and tore her
up   no one
tossed her away

she never saw her roots or knew
the point and
danger of her thorns
                or could have
understood that field of bright
poppies   blood red and
heavy with the sun and
helpless against storm scythe mower heat or the great
pig rooting and trampling her way into the field's
heart
      (the air alive with bees and the whole
field buzzing)

ii. *like a stone*
she grew whole like a
stone and always
smaller   wearing
down to that blind knotted
bit of herself
hard as the rock she'd
worn away from
              and always
smaller and harder till she was
sand
      and dust
           and then she
blew away

iii. *like a strong woman*
she grew whole like a strong
woman
        like a stone
like a rose

                 she is a hand
ful of thorns and contradictions   always
dusty and growing and
wearing away
                      no one owns
her   she is touched by
everything
                 knotted in the deep dry ground and
waving her shreds and tatters under the lovely
sun
       stripped battered
buried again and again and sprouting
up for that familiar
unfamiliar unfolding
an opening
a great shout of colour

nothing is safe
                      she is
sweet and sharp   alive and
dangerous
                 and the dangerous
bees adore her.

Biographical Notes

Dorothy Allison was born in Greenville, South Carolina. She is a lesbian writer and activist who now lives in New Jersey. Her fiction, poetry and essays have appeared in *Conditions*, *The Village Voice*, *Womanews*, *Bad Attitude* and other magazines, as well as *Lesbian Fiction* and *Lesbian Poetry* (Persephone Press), and *Pleasure and Danger* (Routledge & Kegan Paul). Her teaching experience has included classes in Radical Anthropology, Feminist Political Theory, and Women's Writing Workshops. In 1973, she helped found the magazine *Amazing Grace* in Tallahassee, Florida. From 1976 until 1979 she was an editor of the journal *Quest: A Feminist Quarterly*, and from 1981 to 1986 she was an editor of the journal *Conditions*. Her book of poetry, *The Women Who Hate Me*, is available from Firebrand Books, which will also publish her short stories in 1988. She is working on an anthology of erotic fiction and essays, as well as a novel.

Beth Allen is thirty-two, and has lived and worked in London for twelve years. She has wanted to be a writer since she was five, and sold her first illustrated book at the age of six – to her father! More recently she has written a collection of lesbian and gay short stories, as yet unpublished.

Jane Barnes grew up in Fort Bragg, California, and has lived in Boston for the last twenty years. In 1974 she and other writers founded a literary newspaper, *Dark Horse*, which she edited for six years. She is the founder/editor of two presses, Quark Press and Blue Giant Press. Her poems and short stories have been published in *Harvard Magazine*, *Hanging Loose*, *Ploughshares*, *Sojourner*, *Ascent*, *Dark Horse* and other magazines. She has just completed her second poetry collection, *Giving Up*, and is working on a collection of short stories and a novel. She teaches writing privately and lives in Cambridge, Massachusetts.

Judith Barrington grew up in Brighton, and was involved in the Women's Liberation Movement in London from 1972 to 1976, when she moved to the United States. She now lives in Portland, Oregon, where she is a full-time writer, contributing articles on women's issues to newspapers and magazines, and working on her second book of poetry. In 1984, she founded The Flight of the Mind annual week-long writing workshop for women, held annually in Oregon's Cascade Mountains.

Linda Bean: 'I was born in 1960 to white working class parents, who worked very hard to send me to university and so to give me the opportunities I have now. I have three part-time jobs, and spend what little time I have left working at writing. I write poetry, short stories, reviews and articles. I have had work published in *Gen* and *Spare Rib*, and have contributed articles to the forthcoming anthologies *Women and the Media* and *In Other Words: Feminist Writing*. I am currently working on a play.

'I live in London with my two cats and my best friend. I'd like to thank Maud for giving me the encouragement to send off my work to publishers. She is an inspiration.'

Robin Becker lives and works in Cambridge, Massachusetts, where she teaches poetry and fiction writing courses at the Massachusetts Institute of Technology. She serves as Poetry Editor for *The Women's Review of Books*. Her book of poems, *Backtalk*, was published by Alice James Press in 1982. She has published poems in many magazines and anthologies, including *Amazon Poetry*, *Aphra*, *The Antioch Review* and *Harvard Magazine*. Her short story 'In the Badlands' appears in *The Things That Divide Us*, an anthology of stories about relationships between women. Robin was an invited poet at the Third International Interdisciplinary Congress on Women, held in Dublin in July 1986. She is the recipient of a Fellowship in Poetry from the Massachusetts Artists Foundation in 1985–86. She has recently completed a new manuscript of poems entitled *Walking Rain*.

Beth Brant (Degonwadonti) is a Bay of Quinte Mohawk from Theyindenaga Reserve in Deseronto, Ontario. She was born May 6, 1941, married at seventeen, and had three daughters. After she divorced, she attempted the job of raising her children on a high school dropout's unskilled labour. She worked as a salesclerk, waitress, sweeper, cleaning woman and Title IV coordinator. Beth started writing at the age of forty after a trip through the Mohawk Valley, where a bald eagle flew in front of her car, sat in a tree, and instructed her to write. She has been writing since. She is the co-founder of Turtle Grandmother, an archive and library for Native American women, and a clearing-house for their manuscripts, published and unpublished. She lives in Detroit with Diane, her lover of ten years, and two of her children.

Lorraine Bray was born in 1962 and grew up in the High Peak District of Northern England. She works around the representation of women and male violence against women. She has recently returned to farming, where she says she castrates bull calves with fervour. 'Not Out to Get Her' was written on the 236 bus from Ridley Road to Broadway Market in September 1985.

MARIAN RUTH

Olga Broumas lives in Provincetown and teaches at Freehand, a fine arts program for women. She is a licensed bodywork therapist and a musician, and travels widely giving readings and presentations of her work. At Freehand she uses healing and bodywork skills to expand the capacity for memory, ecstasy and expression, and her class provides a forum where the process and preconditions embodied in a work of art can be known and embraced. Recent books are *Black Holes, Black Stockings*, co-authored with Jane Miller, and *What I Love, Selected Translations of Odysseus Elytis*. She is currently at work on his essays.

Roz Calvert is a native Iowan. She lives and works in New York City's Lower East Side, and writes poetry and original screenplays.

Chaucer Cameron: 'I live in the East End of London and am a lesbian feminist mother of a four-year-old son and a twelve-year-old daughter. I have been writing in many forms since I was very young. My dream is to illustrate my work. I spend a lot of time exploring feminism and other things. I would like to move abroad where there is sun and the attitude towards wimmin with children and children individually is less hostile and more healthy. I feel lucky to have been able to come out in surroundings where the tolerance of lesbians is reasonably high and there is a strong lesbian feminist network.'

Andrea R. Canaan, thirty-six, is a Black Southern lesbian feminist, co-mother, poet and writer. Living in Oakland, California when she wrote 'Girlfriends', she now resides in New Orleans, Louisiana, her original home.

Chrystos: 'Born November 7, 1946, in San Francisco. Reside on Bainbridge Island, Washington State. Published in *This Bridge Called My Back*, *A Gathering of Spirit* and various anthologies and periodicals. Currently preparing a manuscript of collected poems for Press Gang in Canada and writing a play, *Rudey Toot Zoo*. My tribal affiliation is Menominee. My political efforts are for the most part devoted to repealing PL 93-531 (Navajo relocation act). My deepest gratitude to the Women of Color Potluck which helps keep me sane.'

Jan Clausen is a writer and activist who lives in Brooklyn, New York. Her books include *Sinking, Stealing* (novel), *Duration* (poetry and prose), *Mother, Sister, Daughter, Lover* (short stories) and *Waking at the Bottom of the Dark* (poetry). She was a founding member of *Conditions* magazine, and in 1981 received a National Endowment for the Arts writing fellowship in fiction. Her reviews of feminist books appear widely. She is co-parent to a sixteen-year-old daughter.

COLLEEN MCKAY

Caroline Claxton: Born 1960. 'I live in London. Writing's not my "job" – who can afford that? I try to get paid for Stage Managing and write when I can. "Lesbian" is about all those stereotypes you know and hate. I got a short story published by The Women's Press (*Girls Next Door*). At the moment I'm still trying to find time to write, but little things like finding work and women's liberation keep getting in the way.'

Janna Davis: Born 1944. 'I have three children, came late in life to feminism, and have since found great strength, affection and sisterhood working for and with women in Women's Aid. A confirmed introvert, I enjoy mostly solitary activities, especially writing and reading.'

Mary Dorcey was born in County Dublin, Ireland, where she was educated at convent school. She has travelled widely, living in England, France, Japan and America, where she worked at a variety of jobs including waitress, caterer, disc-jockey, and English language teacher. She has been active in the Women's Movement since 1972 and was a founder member of Irish Women United. Her work has appeared in journals in Britain, America and Ireland, and she has given many readings. Her first book, *Kindling*, was published by Onlywomen Press in 1982. Since then her work has been anthologised in *Bread and Roses* (Virago), *In the Pink* (The Women's Press), and *Beautiful Barbarians* (Onlywomen Press) among other places. She is currently living in the west of Ireland completing a book of short stories and working on a novel.

Elana Dykewomon is the current editor of *Sinister Wisdom*, author of *Riverfinger Woman, They Will Know Me By My Teeth* and *Fragments From Lesbos*. She is a lesbian separatist, printer, member of the Jewish Lesbian Writers Group, and a partner in Diaspora Distribution. After many wanderings she now lives in Oakland, California, where she often feels like a lemming surprised by the reality of the sea.

© JEB 1982

R.V. BAILEY

U.A. Fanthorpe: 'Born 1929, educated perfunctorily in Surrey and began to learn at Oxford (St Anne's College). After sixteen years teaching I decided I wanted to learn more about myself and the world, and found a job as clerk/receptionist in a small neurological hospital in Bristol. I'd always meant to write, but teaching interfered, whereas low grade hospital work pitched me into poetry. Three books published so far by Harry Chambers/Peterloo Poets, and a fourth due out this year, also a third of a volume of poetry for children (Oxford University Press), and a selection from the three Peterloo collections was published in 1986 as a King Penguin. (The others in the series are all men . . .) I live in Gloucestershire with the woman who has shared my life for the last twenty-one years.'

Eve Featherstone: 'I have been writing for quite a few years now and giving readings to women. I have never tried to publish my work before for two reasons: firstly because my daughter was worried about people finding out that I was a lesbian and giving her a hard time, so if anyone reading this book has any nasty notions about harassing either the contributors or our children – beware . . . The second reason was that I didn't want men reading my stuff and getting off on the lesbian bits, so if any man is reading this to get off on the lesbian bits stick your head or better still your whole self in a bucket of icy water. Anyway, I have now decided to publish my writing so that other working class lesbian mothers who went to secondary modern schools and thought they were stupid because they never learned to mistress spelling let alone sintax can read it (and get off on the lesbian bits).'

Paula Finn works with Art Against Apartheid, and is the director of a literacy project at the Amalgamated Clothing and Textile Workers Union. Her writing has been published in *Ikon*, *Art and Artists* and *Win* magazine. She lives in the Washington Heights section of Manhattan.

Gudrun Fonfa and her lover reside temporarily in Nevada. Her poetry, short stories and essays have been published primarily in feminist publications. She has recently written a television movie on Fat Oppression. Her collection of poems *the poems that write themselves* is almost ready to search for a publisher. She has a daughter in college.

Jane Frances: 'I live alone (cats, potplants) among wonderful friends. I've had various jobs and never (yet?) settled down. I commute between ascetic political rigour and a pastoral fantasy of gardening, books and music, by the sea. I was always writing – secretly. Then I ventured out – rejections. Now here I am!'

Sharon Franklet 'sleeps in a single bed these days and sometimes loves it. In the little bed she doesn't get lost so often like she has in bigger beds in the past. Now, is that an advantage or a disadvantage?'

Kath Fraser: 'Born in London in 1947, I have lived in Colne, Lancashire, for the last six years. Writing is something I grasp and abandon repeatedly – whether in journals, poetry, prose fiction or non-fiction. I am now sculpting a lot of the time as I like stone and hands and touching and space and relationships between forms.'

Jean Freer was born in California in 1945 and emigrated to England in 1968. Politically active as a lesbian separatist, she co-ordinated the fourth National Women's Liberation Conference, originated the Brighton Lesbian Group and helped organise Wise, the women's music festival at Pilton in 1982. She also founded the Feminist Archive. Jean lived at Greenham Common Women's Peace

213

Camp for two years, producing a radical reply to *Breaching the Peace* entitled *Raging Womyn*. Her article 'Gaea: The Earth as Our Spiritual Heritage' was included in The Women's Press anthology *Reclaim the Earth*. Her work has also appeared in such diverse journals as *Catcall*, *Panakaeia*, *Red/Rad Newsletter*, *Feminist Review* and *Arachne*. Her book *The New Feminist Tarot* is published by Thorsons.

Beatrix Gates, born 30 October 1949, has been writing poems since the age of twelve. She designed and printed her first two letterpress chapbooks, *native tongue*, 73 and *Shooting at Night*, 80, both now out of print, and her ms. *Swimmer of Air* is circulating. Most recently, her poems have appeared in *Nimrod*, *Racoon*, and *The Women's Review of Books*. She lives in Brooklyn, New York, and Penobscot, Maine, and works in both places as Designer/Editor/Publisher of Granite Press.

Joan Gibbs is an activist and more recently an attorney who lives and works in New York City. She is the author of one book of poetry, *Between A Rock And A Hard Place*, and is currently working on a collection of short stories, essays and poems, tentatively titled *Bearing Witness*. With Sara Bennett, she collected, published and distributed *Top Ranking: A Collection of Essays on Racism and Classism in the Lesbian Community*. Joan's writings — poems, short stories and articles — have appeared in several publications, among them *The Iowa Review*, *Azalea*, *The Guardian*, and *Win Magazine*.

Janice Gould is a thirty-seven-year-old writer and musician who grew up in Berkeley, California. She is a part-time secretary, working for the Native American Studies Department at UC Berkeley, and a part-time student, working on her M.A. in English at the same institution. Her thesis is on Native American women poets. She is herself Native American, Maidu, a California tribe. She plans to attend the University of New Mexico in the fall of 1987, for a Ph.D in American Studies, continuing her studies in Native American Literature.

Judy Grahn grew up in Chicago, and in southern New Mexico. She has lived in California since 1968. In 1970 she co-founded the first all-women's press which published, printed and distributed a variety of new women's voices, including her own *Edward the Dyke*, *The Common Woman Poems* and *A Woman is Talking to Death*. She currently teaches women's writing, poetry, literature and gay and lesbian studies classes in the Bay Area.

Among her most recent books is *Another Mother Tongue: Gay Words, Gay Worlds* which was chosen by the American Library Association as its Gay Book for the Year in 1985. Her work has been widely translated and anthologised. '

Pamela Gray is a Jewish lesbian writer living in Oakland, California. Her work appears in *New Lesbian Writing and Women-Identified Women*, and will appear in Firebrand Press's forthcoming anthology on lesbian parenting.

Caroline Griffin: 'I was born in 1950 in the Midlands, and have three sisters. For the past thirteen years I have taught English in a South London boys' comprehensive school. I am a "non-biological mother" (or "non-birthical", as my seven year old daughter suggests) – and also committed to all the ways we can mother each other. I've been agoraphobic for years and would like this to change. My mother, Sylvia, died in April 1986. I hope she's glad I'm still writing poetry.'

Marilyn Hacker was born in the Bronx, New York in 1942. She is the author of five books of poetry, including *Assumptions* (Knopf), and *Love, Death and the Changing of the Seasons*, which was published in New York by Arbor House, and will appear in Britain with Onlywomen Press. From 1982 to 1986, she was editor of the feminist literary magazine, *13th Moon*. She lives in New York City and in Paris with her daughter, Iva.

215

Kate Hall: 'I was born in 1945, just after World War Two ended. I came out in 1978. I am working class and a mother. I work teaching dance, movement and writing and as a therapist. I have a teenage daughter Amy, and various animals. I write fiction and poetry, draw and paint whenever I have time. Being a lesbian feminist has been and still is an exciting and positive experience for me, which seems to confuse some people.'

Caroline Halliday: 'I am a white lesbian, a co-mother, a feminist. Our poetry as lesbians must continue to be about taking risks in telling each other more truths about ourselves, exploring our taboos, celebrating our spirituality in our physical selves . . . to confront and establish *who we really are* as lesbians. There isn't time for anything else . . . My poetry collection *Some Truth, Some Change* came out in 1983; and I have poems in *Spinster* Vol 3, *One Foot on the Mountain* (1979), *Hard Words and Why Lesbians Have to Say Them* (1982), *Dancing the Tightrope* (1987), *New British Poetry 1968–88* (1988). I have co-produced a children's book *Everybody's Different* (with Ingrid Pollard), and I have an article about (lesbian) children's books in *In Other Words* (ed Chester and Neilsen 1987). I am writing novels . . .'

Gillian Hanscombe was born in Melbourne, Australia in 1945. She has lived in England since 1969. Her books include *Hecate's Charms*, *Rocking the Cradle* (with Jackie Foster), and *Between Friends*.

Debra Helme: 'I am twenty-four and a vegetarian. I was born in Barbados, brought up in a council house in Preston (with my mum and brother), have been to polytechnic and university, worked as a chambermaid, barmaid, domestic assistant and am currently having a bash at tele-sales (I hope to be sacked quite soon). I also do part-time youth work where I run the weekly disco and conduct my campaign against sexism. I am involved in the setting up of the lesbian centre within the New Women's Centre in Nottingham. My latest fund raising effort was an extremely unsuccessful jumble sale. I like my life to be busy and jam-packed with experiences, and this doesn't leave much time for sitting and writing it all down. I used to write plays on the top of buses, but now I've got a car I find it difficult to hold a pen and the steering wheel at the same time. When I write it comes in spurts. I write plays and poems and am ten pages into my first (autobiographical of course) novel. I doubt it will ever be finished. I live in Nottingham with my cat, Flutel.'

J.P. Hollerith: 'I am a white, middle class lesbian. I was born and raised in Canada. I came to England to continue my academic research and am now a fixture around the place. For many more years than I care to consider I made my home in a cast-iron closet; after some work I transformed myself into a radical feminist dyke. I write science fiction/fantasy and have had a few short stories published in the U.K. and abroad. I work on my local Lesbian Line, do a bit of carpentry, and generally try to create Lesbian Nation by living it now.'

MARG YEO

Joy Howard is in her mid-forties and still not in the business of settling down comfortably, though she is beginning to think this might be nice.

Maria Jastrzebska: 'Born in Warsaw, Poland, I came to England as a small child and grew up in London. Write in English, inspired by Polish, my first language: write poetry because it's short and tries to make its own language. Recently member of lesbian writers' group and local women's writing workshop, I'm now working part time in a school, also teach women's self defence. I have been a lesbian most of my life, active feminist for many years. My work has been published in *Spare Rib*, *Spinster* and *Writing Women*, my translations of the Polish writer Ludwicka Woznicka's stories in *Literary Review* and *Argo*.'

Jenn is a feminist and teacher who spends much of her time trying to impress on adolescent girls that they don't have to get married and have two point five children. Success is rare, but she continues to persevere. She lives in a house by the sea with a friend and a washing machine.

INGRID POLLARD

Jackie Kay: 'I was born in 1961 and brought up in Scotland. My poems have appeared in various anthologies, including: *A Dangerous Knowing, Beautiful Barbarians, Dancing The Tightrope, Black Women Talk Poetry*. I live and work in London, teaching and writing and running various workshops. At the moment I'm working on a collection of poems about adoption.'

Melanie Kaye/Kantrowitz, born Brooklyn, New York, is the author of *We Speak In Code: Poems and Other Writings*, and a forthcoming book on women, violence and resistance; she has published widely in the progressive, Jewish, feminist and lesbian press. From 1983–87 she edited and published *Sinister Wisdom*, a lesbian feminist journal, and, with Irena Klepfisz, co-edited *The Tribe of Dina: A Jewish Women's Anthology*. She teaches writing and women's studies in the Adult Degree Program of Vermont College.

Meg Kelly is a former journalist and now an adult education teacher. She has a son and lives by the sea.

Daisy Kempe has an obsession with windmills and words, and is woman-identified. She works in Canada every summer in order to pay for winters in Cambridge writing poetry. She is currently engaged in two poetry anthologies, called *Dislocations and Roses* and *Postcards and Clowns*, which includes the poem 'Changes'. Between transatlantic trips she attends to her young daughter Kate, and tends her garden of red and yellow roses.

Tina Kendall: 'i am black and a dyke, left-handed, vegetarian, working-class/
i have a son and a lover who's pregnant and i'm partly a "yorkshire lass"/
i like to dance and to write and to dream in the night, and sunsets and rivers and trees/
am allergic to cats, hysterical about rats and writing biographical notes makes me sneeze.'

© DEE CONWAY

Kim: 'Name: Kim aka Terry van Dyke comic poet
Born: London 15 May '61
1st Regret: Being white and middle class
1st Poem: June '71 'Things I Hate'
1st Out: October '83 – Theory becomes practise
1st Performance: Lesbian Strength '84
1st Published: Now
1st Love: Collecting pigs
1st Ambition: Fame . . . while still living!'

© JENNY MCKENZIE

Linda King writes from the perspective that life experience as a black woman choosing love as a foundation from which to live is a story that must be told. Born in Tampa, Florida, on June 27, 1952, she attended Morris Brown Spelman College, and Richmond College, University of London. She has lived in London since 1976, and has two children who reside with their father during the week and with her on weekends. She has worked as a Health Community worker, Playleader Community worker, and Tutor/Development worker, Race Relations and Anti-Racist Staff Development Consultant.

Linda King has been writing for two and a half years. So far she has finished a novel, an essay, three short stories and a volume of poetry.

© PAULA NEILSON

Irena Klepfisz was born in 1941 in Warsaw, Poland, and emigrated to the US in 1949. She grew up in New York City and received her Ph.D in English in 1970. She has taught English, Yiddish, Women's Studies, and numerous writing workshops. A founding editor of *Conditions* magazine, she is the author of *Keeper of Accounts* and *Different Enclosures*. She has written on childlessness, office work, anti-Semitism and Jewish identity and her fiction, essays

219

and poetry have appeared in the lesbian, feminist and Jewish press, most recently in *The Women's Review of Books*, *Lilith* and *Moment*. She has been anthologised in *Nice Jewish Girls*, *Lesbian Fiction*, *Lesbian Poetry* and *Woman Poet: East*. She is co-editor of *The Tribe of Dina: A Jewish Women's Anthology* (Sinister Wisdom Books), and is translating Yiddish women writers as well as experimenting with bilingual Yiddish/English poetry.

Jennifer Krebs: 'I was born on September 27, 1957 in Spencerport, New York. My parents belonged to a reform (Ashkenazi) synagogue where I was Bat Mitzvahed. I now live in San Francisco and when I'm not working at Old Wives' Tales Bookstore, I write stories and poems and belong to Mothertongue Reader's Theater.'

NAOMI BUSHMAN

Joan Larkin has published two collections of poetry: *Housework* (Out & Out Books) and *A Long Sound* (Granite Press). She co-edited (with Elly Bulkin) *Amazon Poetry* and *Lesbian Poetry: An Anthology*, and was a founding member of Out & Out Books, a women's independent press active from 1975 to 1981. She teaches writing in Brooklyn College, and has taught workshops in New York, Maine, Massachusetts, Florida, and at Sarah Lawrence College. She lives in Brooklyn with her daughter, Kate.

MARIAN ROTH

Jacqueline Lapidus was born in New York in 1941. She returned to the United States in May 1985 after more than twenty years abroad, first in Greece, then in Paris. She has been a teacher and translator, and now divides her time between Princeton (Cape Cod) and Boston, where she works as a magazine editor.

Rebecca Lewin is a fiction writer, poet and essayist. Her writing has appeared in *Newsday*, *San Francisco Chronicle*, *New York Native*, *Common Lives/Lesbian Lives*, and other journals. She won the 1985 PEN/NEA Syndicated Fiction Competition, and in 1986 was a speaker on the first National Writers Union (U.S.A.) panel on Gay Writers and the Media.

Audre Lorde was born in New York City in 1934. She received her B.A. from Hunter College and did graduate work for an M.L.S. degree at Columbia University. From 1961–63 she was a librarian for the New York Public Library. Ms Lorde is the author of twelve books, both non-fiction and poetry. She was poet-in-residence at Tougaloo College in Jackson, Mississippi in 1968. She is currently Professor of English at Hunter College in New York City. She is a resident of Staten Island.

Maia: 'I'm forty-one, a single mother living in a small university town with a handful of people I love. I grew up in the suburbs of Los Angeles, when it was still orange groves and clapboard houses. Trees and stones, blackbirds and the moon were (still are) my muses. When I was twelve my first poem seized me: words like bees swarming until the sun came up. That was the night I knew I wanted to be a writer. Many of my poems have been published in journals around the country, and this year I'm working on a collection of short stories.'

Caeia March was born in 1946 of white working class parents on the Isle of Man. She grew up in industrial South Yorkshire, and came to London to university in 1964. She graduated in Social Sciences in 1968. She was married that same year, and later had two sons. Caeia has been living as a lesbian since she left her marriage in 1980. Her sons live with their father, some ten minutes from her rented flat in S.E. London. She now teaches part time in Adult Education for several different London boroughs, and especially enjoys tutoring for creative writing courses with women. She has had several short stories published and some poetry. Her first novel, *Three Ply Yarn*, was published by The Women's Press in 1986, and her second novel, *The Hide and Seek Files*, is forthcoming in 1988.

Judith McDaniel is a writer and political activist who lives in Albany, New York. She has published two books of poems, *November Woman* (Loft Press) and *Metamorphosis and Other Poems of Recovery* (Long Haul Press), and a novel, *Winter Passage* (Spinsters Ink). In the spring of 1987 Firebrand Books published *Sanctuary*, a book of essays and poems which includes her experience of being captured by Contra forces in Nicaragua in August 1985.

SOPHIE KIER

Christian McEwen: 'born London, 1956, grew up in Scotland mostly. Moved to the States in 1979, and now live on the Lower East Side of New York. Have worked as a gardener, construction worker, counsellor, editor, creative writing teacher and (currently) literacy advisor. Keep an obsessive journal and depend enormously and passionately on my friends, a number of whom are included in this book.'

INGE MORATH/MAGNUM

Honor Moore lives and writes in Connecticut and New York City. Her poems have been widely published, and in 1981 she received a Creative Writing Fellowship in poetry from the National Endowment for the Arts. *Mourning Pictures*, her autobiographical verse play, earned her a CAPS Grant from the New York State Council for the Arts in 1976, and is included in *The New Women's Theater, Ten Plays By Contemporary American Women. Leaving and Coming Back*, a chapbook of three long poems, was published by Effie's Press in 1981, and her poem 'Spuyten Duyvil', read by the poet with music by Janet Marlow, is part of the Watershed Cassette, *Take Hands, Singing and Speaking For Survival. Firewalker*, her first full-length collection, will be published soon. She is at work on a biography of her grandmother, the painter Margarett Sargent, to be published by Viking Penguin.

SHAHEEN HAQ

Suniti Namjoshi was born in Bombay, India on 20 April 1941. At present she teaches English at the University of Toronto. Her books include *The Jackass and the Lady* (Calcutta Writers Workshop), *From the Bedside Book of Nightmares* (The University of New Brunswick Press), and *The Conversations of the Cow* (The Women's Press).

Nina Newington: 'I write fiction as well as poetry. I'm currently working on my first novel. I'm English, live in the Lower East Side of New York, make my living as a carpenter. I also teach writing workshops for women. As a recovering alcoholic and an incest survivor, breaking silence, telling the truth, discovering I'm not alone, have saved my life. I want my writing to give the gift of not-aloneness to other people as it's been given to me. Communication feels like a miracle. When I'm writing from the deepest part of myself I'm striking sparks in the night. I can see. I'm learning to do more than survive.'

Pat Parker: From the moment she entered the world three months early, it became clear that Pat Parker was not going to be ordinary, and she never has been. Her sense of differences has taken her across the States and to Europe and Africa. It has motivated her to publish five volumes of poetry, appear in numerous magazines and anthologies, and appear on three record albums.

JOAN E. BIREN

Minnie Bruce Pratt was born and raised in Alabama, and now lives in Washington, D.C. Her first book of poetry, *The Sound of One Fork*, was published in 1981. She co-authored, with Elly Bulkin and Barbara Smith, *Yours in Struggle: Three Feminist Perspectives on Anti-Semitism and Racism*. Her most recent book of poetry is *We Say We Love Each Other*. She is the mother of two teenage sons.

Helen Ramsbottom: 'I'm a writer and poet, ex-printer, reluctant Londoner, and lover of the countryside. At present I work part-time in the London co-operative movement.'

223

Adrienne Rich: Born 1929. Author of thirteen books of poetry and three of prose: most recently *Your Native Land, Your Life* (W.W. Norton, London) and *Blood, Bread and Poetry* (Virago). Living and teaching in California.

Jennifer Rose was born in Evanston, Illinois, in 1959. She has lived in Massachusetts since 1971 where she now works as an editor and typesetter. Her poems have appeared in *The Nation*, *Agni Review*, *Ploughshares* and elsewhere. 'At Dachau With A German Lover' is from a manuscript called *The Old Direction of Heaven*. In 1985 she received a 'Discovery'/The Nation award, and in 1982 was named a PEN/New England 'Discovery'. She is very active in the Peace Movement.

Barbara Ruth was born in Kansas in 1946. She has written two novels which are searching for publishers, in addition to numerous poems and short stories. She is a member of the Jewish Lesbian Writers Group and Wry Cups – a Disabled Women's Reader's Theater – both located in the San Francisco Bay Area.

Sapphire: 'I am a Blk lesbian novelist, short-story writer and poet. I live in New York where I have performed dramatic presentations of my work, and am working on my second novel, *The Last Day of Winter/First Day of Spring*. I have worked as a prostitute, dancer, telephone operator and domestic. Currently I am healthy, happy and inspired. For those of you on that wavelength, I am a Leo with a Taurus moon and Sagittarius rising.'

Susan Sherman is a poet, essayist, and editor of *Ikon* magazine, a feminist cultural journal. In the sixties she was active in the poetry scene in New York, organising and running poetry series. She was poetry editor and theatre critic for *The Village Voice*, and had nine plays produced off-off-Broadway. Awarded a CAPS grant for poetry (1976–77), she has published two collections of poetry and a translation of a Cuban play, *Shango de Ima* (Doubleday). In 1985 she was awarded an Editor's Grant from CCLM (Co-ordinating Committee of Literary Magazines), and in 1986 was a recipient of an Editor's Award from the New York State Council of the Arts. She is currently completing a manuscript of poetry, *The Color of the Heart*, and a book of autobiographical prose.

Linda Smukler was the 1986 winner of the Katherine Anne Porter Fiction Competition sponsored by *Nimrod* magazine, and has published in various publications including *Conditions* and *Ikon*. A graduate of Yale University, she was a runner-up in the 1985 Narrative Poetry Competition sponsored by the *New England Review/Bread Loaf Quarterly*. Linda was a recipient of an Edward Albee Foundation Fellowship in 1985, and has studied with Gloria Anzuldua, Joseph McElroy and Grace Paley.

Kay Stirling: 'Born 1951, England. Lived twenty-four years Melbourne, Australia (suburban working class), the last eleven in London. Feel myself located somewhere between the two (no-man's land!). A lesbian for ten years, with work and personal interests largely in books (four years Sisterwrite Bookshop) and women's writing. My own writing voice emerged fledgling-like with other women's, airborne on mid-seventies sisterhood. Recently, I've focused more on visual directions – weaving, drawing, photography; taking advantage of Adult Education in eighties unemployment. Currently a full-time student in a small middle class town in North Yorkshire. I begin to appreciate the difficulties of lesbian existence outside the city's fringe.'

C. Linden Thorp: Born 1952 in a cottage hospital in a suburb of Manchester. 'I was born with a distinctive voice which I dared not tell people about, and so I used to talk to myself. Then I found a place where my voice was accepted – the world of classical music. I studied at the Royal Northern College of Music, and began to use my voice in writing poems. In 1983 I decided to come alive in the Lake District. I began to write prose for the first time. Nowadays my life is filled with music teaching, which is my occupation, and I am at present in the process of training as a teacher of the Alexander technique. I live in a house of women: Lilly, my amanuensis, Roz, our black labrador, and Jessie and Tooty, our two tortoiseshell pussies.'

Lisa Vice: 'Born 1951. Unknown ethnic origins. Roots buried somewhere among barbers and soldiers, suicides and survivors, assembly line workers and avon ladies, teetotalers quoting scripture and alcoholics glueing rhinestones onto dog collars.'

BRENDA PRINCE

Marg Yeo: was born in Canada and now lives in London. She is the author of *Game for Shut-ins*, *Evolutions*, *the custodian of chaos*, *something about silence*, and *unnatural acts*. In this, her most recent collection of poems, she writes that the works themselves are autobiographies. 'They show me that i've grown up in my feminism, in my lesbianism, and perhaps most importantly in my anger, and they remind me too that they, and i, owe everything we are to other women.'